Confident
&
Credible

Confident & Credible

Presentations so good you deserve applause!

By Gail Zack Anderson

Published by FuzionPrint. 1210 E 115th Street, Burnsville, MN

Printed in the United States of America

Cover Design & Interior Book Design: FuzionPrint

Library of Congress Control Number: 2016944391

ISBN: 978-0-990-9039-8-7

Dedication

For years I dreamed about writing this book. When I finally decided to start, my mother, who was well into her late eighties, became my biggest fan. She always asked how it was going, and often wanted to read what I was writing. It kept me going because, after all, who wants to disappoint your mother? I hope she is smiling down at this, the final product.

With the help of Connie Anderson, a skilled and relentless editor, I made major revisions, moved the chapters to a better sequence, and through her tutoring, learned how to be a better writer. Jean Kindem brought to life the look and feel I wanted. Ann Aubitz of FuzionPrint helped me to "see" what it could look like, and helped me publish it. That meant a lot of patience, hand-holding and follow-up calls.

Finally, to my great friends and colleagues who read and gave me feedback every step of the way, a huge "thanks" for believing in me. Becky Bohm, Patsy Kahmann, Julie Berg, Janae Bower, Tara Bryan, Suzanne Murphy, Kathie Pugaczewski, Kara Sime, and Beth Spencer all fit into this category. I'm blessed.

"I used my skills right away back at the office presenting to the whole company. I had two props, called up volunteers and used two fantastic Power of Threes. Super effective in making my targeted message clear. It really worked. I would love to tell you more about that some day!"

-Business Leader, Manufacturing

"You have given me powerful and valuable tools that I know I will carry with me throughout my career. I feel like the mist has parted and the path to powerful speaking has been made very clear."

-Director of Development

"A quick note to let you know the presentation in Singapore was a success and I am in your debt for helping me. I received very positive comments from three of my colleagues with specific feedback that included: well organized, confident, topic expert, and collegial. Further, one of the attendees behaved as predicted and I dealt with him appropriately. Thank you."

-Corporate Audit

"My presentation went very well!! My supervisor even commented on how complete and informative it was without being too much. Great discussions came from the topic. I'm almost sad I don't get to present more often."

-Team Lead

Contents

Foreword

I have worked with Gail Zack Anderson since the turn of the millennium – seems like a long time ago right? Well it was only 16 years ago, and in that time I have seen what a difference her experience in presenting, training and coaching has made for me personally and for others in organizations. I have hired Gail to share her confidence and presentation secrets with individuals and teams. Now many of her workshop secrets are here in this book for anyone to use and refer back to again and again. Gail's practical advice will strengthen and support you, the reader, as you move into public speaking, presenting, and training.

Gail coaches people to develop their strengths. One of the biggest "ah-ha's" I hear from participants is how their presentation nerves don't show through on video as much as they think when first presenting. Once learners take time to listen to feedback about the talents they bring to the presentation they increase confidence and feel more credible. This book will now allow presenters to reflect, read real examples of how others overcame obstacles, and will provide useful actions to build upon the unique talents they bring to the job. Who doesn't want to turn nerves into power, create a clear message, bring content to life, present with impact, and be brilliant? Each chapter of **Confident and Credible** expands on these ideas and more to coach you and support your presentations.

Why you should read this book? Gail Zack Anderson's approach works. The Targeted Message Model in chapter 2 is simple and helps me organize my scattered thoughts. For me, this model has brought focus to complex topics I needed to present. I have also used the tool to develop whole meeting agendas – plan out supervisor training or full day workshops which are built on a theme or targeted message. How does it work? The model helps provide focus by forcing a single thought which gets broken into small segments with bulleted examples, stories, and facts. It helps me eliminate unneeded or tangential topics and ideas to keep things more concise and meaningful. Chapter 2 has been critical for me and my work.

In the past, I used to bring in way too many details, too much 'proof' about what I am trying to say or convince people but really, less is more. Presentations are like planning a wedding. Only the bride (and maybe the mother of the bride) know what is supposed to happen at the event. Out of all the details, no one will notice the few ancillary ones if they get missed, left out or messed up. Training and presenting are just like 'the big day' – only you know what is supposed to be said or what is supposed to happen. When trying to convince someone of your competence or new idea, don't over-do it or look desperate to show how much you know. Give the key details concisely with one or two supporting facts or stories and save a few more details for discussion later. This book helps provide focus as we strive for clarity, confidence and credibility.

Gail is a polished speaker, engaging presenter and encouraging teacher. **Confident and Credible** will extend her skills as a writer to reach a much wider audience across the globe.

Kara Sime – Human Capital Director

Introduction

This book, *Confident and Credible: Presentations so Good You Deserve Applause*, will provide you a step-by-step plan for creating and delivering your best-ever presentations, very much like the coaching sessions and workshops I deliver.

How to use this book

I encourage you to work on an actual presentation as you read the chapters, especially if you will be speaking in the near future. Or, you might choose to work on a typical presentation, or challenge yourself by working on the driest or most difficult presentation you have to give. You can start at the beginning and move from chapter to chapter, or you can jump in wherever you want, depending on where you want to begin.

As a presentation coach and workshop facilitator for more than 25 years, I have come to appreciate the courage it takes for some of us to stand and deliver in front of others, despite our fear and uncertainty. I believe that each of us has a voice and a message to be shared, and with some practical skills and valid feedback we can each learn to create and deliver successful presentations. Whether you are a complete novice, or a seasoned speaker looking for a few pointers to become even better at presenting or training, you will find inspiration as well as practical advice in these chapters. I wish you every success.

Chapter 1: Create a Clear Message

Let's begin at the beginning. By learning to use the Targeted Message Model, you will be able to create compelling themes and targeted messages for your presentations—with less stress and in less time. You will learn how to analyze your audience in order to build a focused presentation.

Chapter 2: Craft Your Content and Bring It to Life

When you have a strong foundation for your presentation, we will examine ways to build meaningful content, decide what level of detail is appropriate, and learn ways to bring your content to life. You will determine an action plan for creating compelling content at just the right level.

Chapter 3: Open and Close for Impact

First, focus on building a great opening to capture your audience's attention, while building your confidence when you need it most. Then work on closings to increase your impact and move the audience to action. You craft your content, opening, and closings.

Chapter 4: Rehearse for Success

When your content is in order, we will explore successful rehearsal tactics, and discover ways to build great rehearsal habits. We will discover ways to learn your content in less time, without memorizing everything. You will be able to create an action plan for your own rehearsal success.

Chapter 5: Be Brilliant with Visuals

Much if not most of the time, your presentations will include visuals of some sort, most likely PowerPoint slides. We will examine best practices in design, content, and delivery of your material with slides. You will learn some simple but effective shortcuts and PowerPoint tricks.

Chapter 6: Engage and Respond

Now we turn to your audience. We will focus on engaging and involving your audience, asking questions to foster discussions, and responding to questions—including challenging ones. You will learn and practice using a Neutral Bridge to help keep your cool—and focus—under fire.

Chapter 7: Turn Nerves to Power

Now is the time to begin thinking of bringing this presentation to your audience. Whether nerves are an annoyance or a huge stumbling block, you will learn techniques you can use to tame the butterflies, including physical, mental, and practical solutions. You will create an action plan and an affirmation to use any time stage fright gets in your way.

Chapter 8: Finding Your Delivery Strengths and Blind Spots

Now that you have your message, your content and your slides ready to go, you will want to be able to express confidence and still feel like yourself. To do that, you need to know what your communication strengths are, those things you do well automatically and easily. You will also want to be aware of blind spots and weaknesses so they don't get in your way. You will do a thorough analysis of your presentation skills.

Chapter 9: Deliver with Style

It's the moment of truth; you are about to step out and deliver your presentation. You'll want to know that you have the skills and habits to maximize your impact. What do you do with your hands? How well does your face project confidence and warmth? Here you will use a checklist and the help of a video recording or live audience to help you "see" your strengths and weaknesses in action, and begin building skills and habits that work for you.

Chapter 10: Speaking Virtually Via Technology

Because so many presentations are done through technology, you'll want to learn how to ace any virtual presentation. Conference calls, virtual team meetings, webinars, teleseminars, or virtual book tours require a slightly different approach to be successful. You will discover ways to connect with your virtual audience, and how to be sure technology is your friend.

We end our journey with a look back at how far you have come and with final thoughts on how you can keep improving and fine tuning. You will put all the pieces together, and prepare to deliver a presentation *so good you deserve applause.*

Chapter 1: Create a Clear Message

Bill was a bright, up-and-coming sales manager in a manufacturing organization. He was good at his job; experienced, smart and confident. At least he was until his boss asked him to present in front of his peers, or to the firm's upper leadership. The minute he heard about an upcoming presentation, he began to worry about what he was going to say, and how he was going to say it. Just when he began organizing his thoughts —Bam!—he was pulled back into meetings, obligations, and busy schedules. Unfortunately, he ended up scrambling to throw the presentation together at the last minute, desperately wishing he had started sooner, and not feeling at all well-prepared.

When Bill and I began working together on his presentation skills, we realized he needed a better, and faster, way to organize his presentations. We first worked at getting focus on the big picture, the essence of the presentation. Once he began to crystallize his thinking, he was able to determine just what content needed to be included, and which he could leave out. His big-picture message provided a framework for the entire presentation, making it easy for Bill to feel excited instead of worried. As a result, he spent much less time putting his presentations together, and less time worrying about the details.

Do you ever feel like Bill? If you do, you are not alone. Busy as we are, no wonder it is difficult, if not impossible, to sit down and thoughtfully plan a presentation. But without careful preparation, we can feel, as well as come across, as scattered and unfocused, and we certainly run the risk of appearing nervous or unprofessional.

And the answer is: the Targeted Message Model

The Targeted Message Model is a systematic method for thinking and preparing content for any presentation. You begin by analyzing your situation, your audience, and your intent for the presentation. You use your analysis to create a one-sentence overview—or Targeted Message. You then build your content around this message, ensuring your content is focused and relevant.

> **❝❝** The Targeted Message helps you focus on what is important, and tells your audience what to listen for, what they should do, and what to remember.

The Targeted Message also informs the beginning, ending, and overall theme for the presentation. We know people tend to remember what they hear first and last, and this process makes sure what they remember *is your message*—instead of some interesting tidbit or isolated fact.

Typical organizational methods

Do you write a script? Create an outline? Or just wing it? You have undoubtedly used one or more of these preparation methods in the past. The trouble is each of them has one or more fatal flaws. As you see in the table below, none of them resolves the problem of how to organize and deliver strategically and effectively. With the Targeted Message

16

Model, you get the best of each of these organizational methods without the drawbacks.

The Targeted Message Model helps you:

- Think strategically before diving into the details.
- Clarify and articulate the purpose of your presentation.
- Focus on what is most important to your listeners.

Because of its modular nature, the Targeted Message Model allows you to create your presentation in stages, so you can work on it while you are in the car, or taking a few moments between meetings. Best of all, creating a new presentation will take less time and be less stressful.

There are various ways to organize your presentation, each of which has advantages and disadvantages. For example, writing a script gives us the ultimate in control, but is time-consuming and difficult to do well. Winging it takes no time, but gives us inconsistent results. By combining the best of these methods, we can have the advantages without the drawbacks. This is what the Targeted Message Model provides you.

	Pros	Cons
Script/Text	• High control	• Time consuming • Difficult to write • Difficult to rehearse • Comes across as unnatural • No flexibility
Outline	• What we are used to doing • Logical • Organized	• Little Flexibility • Difficult to understand by listening • No transitions • No "big picture"
Wing it	• Less prep time • Spontaneous	• Inconsistent • Rambling • Lose control • Illogical • Difficult to follow
Tell 'em	• Gives a good overview • Helps audience to listen	• Does not give enough structure to the body of presentation
Targeted Message Model	• High control • Easy to get used to • Logical • Organized • Less prep time • Elements of spontaneity	

• Gives a good overview
• Helps audience to listen understand and remember

Like any good tool, the Targeted Message Model is flexible.

- If you tend to think visually, you might like to draw your presentation out like a mind map, using the graphic below or a blank sheet of paper.
- If you tend to be more linear and detailed, you might like to use our worksheets or electronic format to write the presentation in a more logical progression.
- If you are working with a team, you might talk it out loud, or draft it on a whiteboard.

Whatever format you like, the elements of the model help you to communicate the big picture, before moving into the details. And it gives you the flexibility to make your presentation more or less detailed, and to shorten or lengthen it as needed.

Elements of the model include:

Targeted Message: the main theme, idea, or point of your

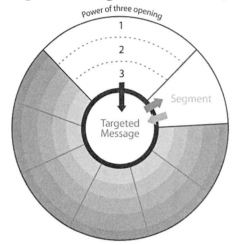

presentation—this one sentence provides a focused beginning and ending to your presentation and ties all the content together.

Segments: major sections or chunks of content which comprise the body of the presentation. This may be similar to an outline, but is not necessarily linear.

Bullets: content and supporting detail or explanation for each segment. This includes the facts, statistics, stories and discussion questions you plan to include.

Transitions: connecting phrases used to move into a segment, and back to the Targeted Message. These help ensure flow and connection between the segments of your presentation.

"Power-of-Three" Opening: an introduction or opening to your presentation built upon three similar phrases, questions, or sentences. You can add it to a more formal presentation, or skip it for a team meeting or informal presentation, starting instead with the message.

Benefits of using a Targeted Message: The beauty of a Targeted Message is that once you capture your message, your entire presentation is focused—targeted to the audience, and their concerns and needs. It's about them, not you. With a powerful message, you can approach the presentation with confidence, knowing you have an important message, and the words to express it. This is a great way to start because it:

- Provides focus and clarity to your presentation
- Creates a meaningful beginning and ending for your presentation
- Helps you determine which details can be safely eliminated
- Sells your idea by stating or implying "what's in it" for the audience
- Improves audience retention

How to create a Targeted Message

Don't spend your time staring at a blank screen, and don't avoid preparation altogether. Instead, start by answering the following five questions to analyze the situation and your audience. Condense your answers to a one-sentence Targeted Message, thereby telling your audience what you are speaking about—and why they should listen.

5 Big Questions to Create a Targeted Message	
1. **Who are you speaking to?**	Who is your audience? Internal or external? How many will there be? Do you know them? What do you know about them? What is the makeup of your audience?
2. **What do you want to say?**	What do you want to say about your topic? Why do you think it is important? What solutions or recommendations do you have? (You may or may not be able to say this directly, but it helps if you are clear about what you think.)
3. **What do they want to hear?**	What is the audience's point of view? How much do they already know, what do they want, what are they feeling, and what objections will they have? What is their emotional state of mind?
4. **What strategies can make your message more acceptable?**	What strategies can you use to make your message attractive or compelling? Should you use logic, data, or emotion? Or some combination of these? Why should they listen? Why should they agree with you, or accept your recommendation?
5. **What outcomes do you want?**	What do you want to happen as a result of this presentation? What specifically do you want the audience to do? Think? Feel? Or remember?

> " *An effective Target Message is specific to the audience, the time and place, and feels just right when you say it. It's what you would say if you only had a minute to speak.*

Sometimes this process is simple and speedy. Other times it takes longer, especially when your presentation is complex. But when you feel clear about the answers, you should be able to create a single sentence to capture the essence of your analysis, and you can also use it to begin and end your presentation. *Try to get it down to one sentence.* Not a question, not a title, but a clear, complete thought, to ensure the audience will understand it and its context. (They don't have to agree, which will come after your presentation.)

If the sentence is too long, you may be able to edit out unnecessary introduction or background until you have a fairly streamlined message—around 25–35 words is a good range. Some Targeted Messages are shorter, some are longer, but it should be more than a slogan, and less than a paragraph.

Say your Targeted Message out loud. Do you like your sentence structure, your choice of words? Will it grab and hold your audience? Will they want to hear more? If the answer is yes, you can use this message to start building the rest of your presentation.

If not, keep at it. Walk away, and then come back. Talk to someone who knows your situation. Doodle, sketch, or make a mind map. Take a walk. Try again. Often the right message comes to us once we stop trying to force it. Grab a pen or pencil and write down your message, then edit and polish it, and you will be ready to build the rest of the presentation. See below for a few examples demonstrating the look and feel of a good Targeted Message:

Sample Targeted Messages

"At the end of this training you will have learned and practiced several techniques you need to close more sales, and to make more money— starting today."

"Upgrading our lab equipment will save us money in the short term, and allow us to postpone purchasing new until we move to the new plant."

"Despite uncertainties in the market, investing your retirement funds in a balanced portfolio will help you save for a comfortable retirement."

"If you want to connect with your customers in real time—provide them incentives to purchase, and establish yourself as a responsive partner— consider creating and contributing regularly to a blog."

When you begin using Targeted Messages to create compelling presentations, you won't want to do it any other way. It gives you control and confidence at the beginning and end of each presentation, and it saves you time and worry when putting your presentations together.

Test your Targeted Message

Make sure it is a complete sentence. Because the idea is to have this one important sentence scripted, write it exactly as you would say it. Don't make it a question, a topic, or a subject.

Make sure it stresses benefits. You will want your message to contain benefits or positive outcomes for the audience, the team, or the organization. Even if these should be obvious, it never hurts to remind the listeners "what's in it for them." Doing this provides a good incentive to listen.

Make sure your audience will understand the message and its context. Take a moment to set the scene. Why is this important now? Be careful about using too many acronyms, technical terms or jargon. If everyone understands, it's no problem, but for anyone who doesn't, this is the kiss of death. If they don't understand your message, they definitely won't understand your presentation, which defeats the purpose.

Make sure you feel comfortable. It is critical that you feel comfortable with the message, as well as the exact words you choose to express it. The Targeted Message should make you feel good every time you say it. If it doesn't, go back to the drawing board. Keep playing with those five key questions, as well as the wording of your message, until you like it. If you like it and believe in it you will be more likely to say it with conviction. Watch out if someone else told you what the message should be—it is better and easier to use your own words.

Check the length. Your message should be limited to one main idea, and consist of around 25–30 words for a routine or simple presentation, and up to about 45 words for a more comprehensive one. You should be able to say it in one breath without tripping on the words. Say it out loud to discover if it flows easily. Say it again. If it's too long, you may stumble; too short, and it might be no more than a slogan or catch phrase.

You will notice sometimes creating a Targeted Message is effortless, and it seems to appear like magic. Other times, you struggle with your thoughts and your words. Consider walking away for a little while to clear your head, and then come back to it. Or find someone who can talk it out with you.

Creating your Targeted Message

Think of a presentation you are currently working on, or a presentation you give regularly, and answer the following questions. This helps you analyze the situation, audience, and your goals, as well as any underlying concerns or hidden agendas. Next, write a Targeted Message, a single sentence which is the theme or main message for your presentation.

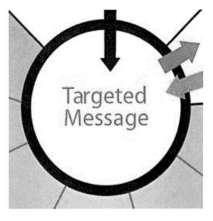

Remember, the five questions are strictly for you, but the Targeted Message will be spoken out loud to your audience.

Create your Targeted Message

1. Who are you speaking to?

2. What do you want to say?

3. What do they want to hear?

4. What strategies can make your message more acceptable?

5. What outcomes do you want?

Draft your Targeted Message

When you have a good idea about your message, capture the word flow before you forget it. It's okay to keep fine-tuning it, but at some point, get those words down on paper, or your smart phone or laptop—whatever method is convenient to capture them. If you don't capture your main message, you may lose it, and *this part* of your presentation should always be planned—stated clearly, and remembered.

Your Targeted Message might change as you continue to reflect upon your presentation, or as new information comes to light. You might also find it useful to discuss your Targeted Message with someone you trust. Keep revising until it accurately reflects your goals for your presentation.

What to do about a "bad news" message

Sometimes your presentations contain bad news: We didn't make the numbers. We didn't improve customer satisfaction. There was an accident in the plant. We didn't win the new business.

When it happens, decide if the bad news is the Targeted Message, or if the bad news is another detail to the larger picture. Again, what is the main message you want the audience to take away and remember? Today's results…or the effort being made to bring results closer to projections?

When you are faced with giving a bad-news presentation, take time to fully analyze the situation. You may be uncomfortable, knowing your audience may resist or disagree with you. Take a little extra time formulating and testing your Targeted Message, and consider getting a second opinion before proceeding.

Whenever possible, focus on solutions, instead of problems or blame. You could sandwich the bad news with the future direction you plan to take. For example, "Although we missed this month's inventory targets, the actions we took should put us in good shape next month."

Use neutral or passive language to create distance from bad news. Instead of stating, "We messed up," you might say things like, "We experienced a setback." Normally this would be too neutral for a Targeted Message, but in this case it does create a buffer zone.

Don't try to hide the bad news, or obscure it with technical detail. Sometimes we beat around the bush, hoping no one will notice the bad news. Other times we dwell on it, and forget the lessons learned, or the positive path we are on now. Find the balance between ignoring bad news, and focusing too much on it. Keep your message clear and simple.

Chapter Recap:

1. Spend time analyzing your situation, your goals, and your audience. Be as clear as you can in each of these areas.
2. Talk it out, or take notes. Research your audience, if needed.
3. Write a one-sentence statement incorporating your thinking, which you will use to begin and end your presentation.
4. Using the test questions in the chapter, test your message, and say it out loud. This is the heart of your presentation, and you will build the rest of your content around it.

Chapter 2: Craft Your Content, and Bring It to Life

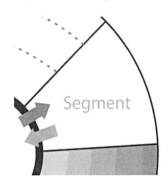

Once you have created an effective Targeted Message, you will probably feel a great sense of relief. You have captured the heart and soul of your presentation. Enjoy the moment. Then begin to build the content, segment by segment. How?

Outline it. One way is to simply list the topics or segments you want to discuss in your presentation. This is essentially your outline, and it works well when you are familiar with the content. Outlines tend to be very linear, and you may begin to feel stuck with the sequencing instead of focusing on the connections. This makes it more challenging to do last-minute changes.

Instead, you should be able to connect each segment directly to your message, knowing the actual sequence is less important than making the connections clear. For example, in making a case for purchasing a new plant, should you talk first about benefits—or costs? Your initial thought might be to discuss benefits first, but the right answer depends on your audience. If they always want to talk cost first, maybe that is the better sequence.

Map it. Another way is to draw a mind map of your presentation, with spokes going out from your Targeted Message, one for each segment, and with sub points connected to each segment. If you are a visual learner, you might prefer this style. I encourage people to instinctively begin to draw right on the model. It might help you see the whole of the presentation, which doesn't work as well with an outline.

Question it. A good way to think about segments is by predicting the questions people might ask about your message or subject matter. Let's say you are proposing new software for accounting, and your listeners don't know much about it. They might ask things like:

- What is it?
- Why do we need it?
- Where will we get it?
- How will we transition to it?
- What will it cost?
- When will we implement it?

Often these questions will create a framework for your presentation's segments.

Note it. If you can't easily see patterns in your data, another way to segment it would be to take all the content, facts, data, ideas, numbers or whatever, and write them on sticky notes or three by five cards. Then do a card sort, or move the sticky notes around until you have found natural groupings. These could very well be your segments. This way is a bottom-up approach, and can start you down the path of *detail* over *big picture*, so check back to your Targeted Message from time to time to ensure you aren't going off-track. If you are, you might need to broaden your message to fit the content, or narrow your content by eliminating "stray" details.

Budget your time. When you have decided on which segments fit into your presentation, you can estimate the time you have available for each one. Often you will find three to six segments are a reasonable number to handle in a presentation, and segments will generally take one to ten minutes each to discuss. So, for a five-minute presentation, you might have only two segments of two minutes each, plus an opening and closing. For a one-hour presentation, you might have six segments of seven to nine minutes each. Of course some segments will be longer and some shorter, but you can get a good estimate of your time by looking at the number of segments.

If you find your presentation has 15–20 segments, no matter how long the presentation is, it is going to sound disjointed and confusing. See if you can regroup your segments so you have three to six larger segments. Maybe you will need to leave some less-critical information out, or include it as a follow-up or handout.

It is easy to try to do too much in the time and attention span we are allowed. Looking at the segments as an overview of your presentation can help you stay on track, budget your time, and keep your presentation's scope realistic.

Transitions between segments

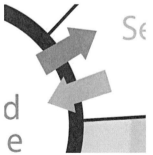

Many of us worry over making transitions in our presentations. Writing a script in order to build transitions is fine if you are crafting a very important speech or writing an article, but for everyday presentations, you may not want to or be able to devote so much time to transitions. However, we still need to get from Point A to Point B, hopefully with a little bit of polish.

Simple transitions help you segue to new information, and create "flow" in your presentation. On the graphic of the Targeted Message Model, you can see the arrows leading toward a new Segment, and the arrows leading back to the Targeted Message. These transitions let the audience know where you are going in your presentation, as well as where you have been.

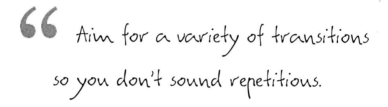

> Aim for a variety of transitions so you don't sound repetitious.

Examples of transitions:

- "What are some of the alternatives to this proposal?"
- "Let's examine alternatives to this proposal."
- "This slide details some of the alternatives to this proposal."
- "Consider some of the alternatives to this proposal."
- By using the specific words, "alternatives to this proposal," you let the audience know what's coming as you transition to new content.

Details, details

How detailed should your presentation be? While there is no single answer to this question, in my experience, it could be a lot less detailed than you think. Many of us think we need to tell the audience everything we know. This is not only impossible; it would be *very boring.*

Some speakers begin by writing text or a script, then reducing it to bullets before delivery. This is very time-consuming, and should be reserved for presentations on brand-new content, or unusual situations. For example, you might be presenting at a conference, or on a panel, something you don't do very often. Then scripting makes more sense. More often, especially when you know your material very well, you will find it faster to start from bullets, and then add a few key details.

Creating your detailed content from bullets can save you lots of time, help you focus rather than memorize, and in the end it will be easier for you to speak from bullets rather than a script.

Tips for using bullets/details:

- Use parallel structure. Start each bullet with a noun or a verb. For example, in this list, all bullets begin with a verb.
- Use bullets in place of numbers when possible, because numbers are difficult to remember, and are often unnecessary.
- Maintain a cryptic style—key words or key ideas. Go back and eliminate unessential words.

Transitions to the Targeted Message or to the next Segment

Transitions create flow, reinforce your Targeted Message, and help keep your presentation on track. You don't need to restate every bullet and detail; simply make a general statement to remind the audience what they have just heard.

Be mindful not to use the words "in closing" or "in summary" as a transition. When you use these words, the audience will think you are concluding your presentation, and they get ready to pack up and leave the room, both physically and mentally.

Transition examples:

"Now that we have looked at several ways of reducing paperwork, let's turn our attention to...."

"When you look at all the alternatives we examined, and ultimately rejected, you can see why we chose the proposal now before you."

"So, as you see, the cost of this new software package will be quickly offset by the improvements in productivity it will help us achieve."

Once upon a time: incorporating stories into your presentations

As he stood up to introduce himself, Greg had a mischievous smile. "I grew up on a little farm in the middle of Iowa, and life wasn't easy," he started. He went on to use his farming background to describe the kind of adult he had grown up to be. How he had learned about responsibility. How he had experienced the satisfaction of hard work, sometimes with little reward. The audience sat in rapt attention to what could have been a routine introduction.

Greg had already discovered the power of stories. Stories can pull us in, tugging at our imaginations or curiosity. We want to hear what happened. What was the problem? How was it resolved? Did everyone live happily ever after?

Many of my clients are scientists, engineers, and accountants. They are always interested in making their content more compelling, but when I mention storytelling as a technique, I sometimes get a funny look. It's as if they are saying, "What? You mean I should tell a story while giving a presentation? You're kidding, right?" They aren't at all sure why or how to use storytelling techniques in their presentations.

It is likely that you too have heard you should use stories to bring your content to life, but you may not be sure how to do it. You might wonder if using stories is worth the risk of looking silly, or worth the time it will take to learn to do it well.

Here are some of the compelling reasons why I think it is worthwhile to use stories and storytelling in your presentations:

Stories make your presentations more interesting. Sure, numbers and statistics are fascinating to some of us, but not everyone thinks so. Adding a story can bring the numbers to life, and make them more compelling. For example, don't just dwell on dollars during a fundraiser, but include human-interest stories about why the money is important to the people involved.

Stories engage the audience. It is pretty easy to daydream through a data-driven or technical presentation, but when a story begins, we get drawn in. Think about watching a boring television program, when all at once the advertisement appears. Advertisements use story, dialog, character, sounds, and music to tell the story. You are drawn into the story despite yourself.

Stories increase retention. We remember very little in the way of facts and details, only about ten percent or so of what we hear. But stories engage our emotions and our senses, so we tend to remember them better. If you doubt it, think back to some of the stories you loved as a child, and see how much you can remember. Or do the same with a favorite movie. Now, compare your feelings to the last meeting you attended. My guess is you actually can recall more of the old story or movie than you can the new content, without a story.

Stories can add a touch of humor. You may not be able to tell a joke, and perhaps you shouldn't, but you can add personal interest and humor. Choose true stories or anecdotes that always get a good laugh, and can help illustrate a point you are making. In stories, you can be silly or playful, and it is okay because it is part of the story.

Stories can be motivating; we can learn from others' mistakes. Many of my clients deliver mandatory safety training. For their audience, this is content they have heard time after time. All the data in the world won't help if it goes in one ear and out the other. But insert a story about something that went wrong, or almost went wrong, and it makes us perk up our ears. We learn the lesson vicariously, and it sticks.

Stories can set the tone. When you open with a story, you send a powerful signal indicating your presentation is going to be different—more interesting and more engaging. Particularly when your content is perceived as dry or difficult, you raise the bar compared to the average presenter.

But can you do it?

You may not consider yourself a "natural" storyteller, but don't sell yourself short; maybe you simply haven't developed this skill yet. You can definitely learn to use stories effectively and appropriately.

The first step in telling stories in your speaking is to find a good story. You probably have many great stories and experiences to share. Telling your own personal stories is a great place to start. They will probably be easier for you to remember, and because they are associated with your own real feelings, it will be easier to bring them to life.

> If you can't think of a story from your own memory bank, don't worry; there are plenty of other places to find them.

Here are places to find stories you can use:

1. Your own experience growing up, on the job, at school, etc.
2. Experiences of your audience, past audiences, co-workers, family, friends, kids, pets, etc.
3. Observation
4. Presentations by other people
5. Books, magazines, web sites
6. Movies, old or new
7. TV shows, talk shows, game shows
8. Fairy tales, fables, nursery rhymes

9. Music lyrics, songs, jingles, rhymes, poems
10. Elders, mentors

Tips and strategies to tell stories

Once you have stories in mind, the next step is building the skills required to tell a story effectively. Make sure you use the story in a way that adds value to your presentation. Tips for story telling:

Use a story to illustrate a point. Use stories to drive home your message, not just as adornment for your presentation. Make the connection clear between your story and the point you are making.

Draw from first-hand experience. Because these stories are authentic, they will ring true. And it will be easier for you to remember all the rich detail surrounding the event.

Keep your story short. Long, drawn-out stories are irritating, especially in a business presentation. Keep them short and sweet. Edit and rehearse until the story can be told in one to two minutes.

Use a story to find common ground. Chose stories your audience can relate to, stories about growing up, high school, cars, first-job experiences, college life, or most embarrassing moments. Remember your audience may have had different experiences than you, so try to draw from universal themes.

Rehearse and time your story. First practice adding description until the story comes to life. It will probably be too long, so then start editing unnecessary detail until you can tell it in one to two minutes.

Don't always make yourself the star. Sharing war stories or stories "all about you" can be a huge turn-off, and simply antagonize your audience. Make them universal stories with a message. Or share your more humbling stories.

Humor: Make 'em laugh

Using humor in business presentations is so tricky some of my clients say things like, "Gail, we don't encourage humor around here. It's too risky in our industry." Yes, bad humor is risky and foolish. But the right use of humor can be magical.

In order to find the perfect blend of serious content and a light touch of humor, you will need to understand your own abilities, your industry, your audience, and your purpose.

First, think about your own skills and natural humor style, and be honest. Are you the life of the party when socializing with friends? Or do you flub the punch line of any joke you have ever told? Or are you the person who thinks he or she is funny, but no one laughs? Ouch! If you aren't sure, ask someone you trust to tell you the truth.

People say everyone has a sense of humor of one type or another. Are you funny with words? Quick with the one-liners? If so, be a little careful—you could easily say something spontaneously which was meant to be humorous, but in hindsight wasn't such a good idea—especially in front of your bosses' boss, or your best customer.

Do you have a wry, dry sense of humor? Does your subtle humor cause a chuckle or a smile? To those who know you, this could be endearing; to others it could be off-putting or seen as sarcasm or negativity.

Are you able to be self-deprecating in a funny way? Be careful you don't put yourself down too much when laughing at yourself.

You see, humor is tricky, especially when stakes are high, and your nerves are on high alert. Always consider your purpose. If this is a serious topic, the lightest touch of humor, especially at the beginning, could be highly effective. But if you have an emotional crowd—layoffs are coming, business conditions are deteriorating, a top exec is in trouble in the media—don't even try to use humor. If you are presenting in order to win new business, a warm and friendly style might be better than a humorous one. But if you are training in the classroom for several hours or perhaps days, look for a few ways to interject humor, for a change of pace, if nothing else.

> " Opt for humor that matches your personal style and feels natural. Be sure it also works for the audience and the occasion.

Start with some very small attempts at humor, and see how they go. Some ways to begin experimenting with humor might include these:

Start small. Tell one short, funny story you think makes a valid point in your presentation. Keep it short and tie it to the point you are making. See how your audience reacts before going for more.

Know your audience. If you know your audience well enough, you can be a pretty good judge of how the humor will go over. Do they appreciate a little humor, or do they prefer to get right to business? If you don't know your audience well, tread carefully until you see how they react. One way I will test the waters with an unknown audience is to ask them a little bit about themselves, and then see how many provide humorous answers.

Keep it short. The one-liner is better than an elaborate joke requiring detailed setup, sequencing, build-up, and punch line. The best stories take a minute or two at most. If your humor is eating up valuable time, your audience probably won't appreciate it.

Look for humor in-the-moment opportunities. Find the humor naturally happening around you, and put it to use. One day I couldn't get my slide remote to work right. It was because I was holding it *upside down*. I made a little quip about "equipment malfunction," but stopped short of apologizing or calling myself "equipment challenged."

Play with words, exaggeration, or timing. Make up your own words, exaggerate your pauses, or make a funny face. Watch comedians or your favorite funny relative to see how they get the laugh. Sometimes it isn't what you say, as much as how you say it.

Don't offend. Any humor making fun of anyone else can and probably will backfire. Everyone loves jokes about lawyers, right? Well, no. Not lawyers, or their families, or friends. Or someone who has had need of one. Same is true of most jokes and much humor. Be cautious—who or what is being laughed at?

Don't tell jokes. Jokes are often offensive because someone is typically the brunt of the joke, like mother-in-law jokes, wife or husband jokes, or blond jokes. Never make fun of anyone's religion, race, nationality, or gender. We used to say, only tell jokes about animals so you won't offend anyone. Guess what? Putting down animals offends many people. My advice is: *don't tell jokes*; find another way to inject humor. Save the jokes for another time and place.

Use a cartoon. A cartoon often captures a normal or absurd thought, and then exaggerates it to make it funny. They often deal with universal themes or unusual characters. The beauty of a cartoon is there is less pressure on you to create the laugh. You show it, and see if it gets a chuckle. Caution: be aware of copyright laws, and seek permission before using someone else's cartoon. If you can draw, create your own.

Use a quotation. Quotations can be touching, or profound, or funny. Sometimes who said it is what makes it interesting. You can find great quotes online.www.QuoteGarden.com. If you are using a quotation, provide attribution whenever available.

Hone your humor. Take an improv or acting class. Go to a comedy club. Try a joke out after work with friends or at home. Read funny material, and play with pacing and pauses. Look for cartoons that make you chuckle. Collect quotations.

Seek feedback as you begin to try out your newfound humor skills. Is it working, or are you trying too hard? Remember humor is like makeup: it is best to use a light touch.

Ways I could bring my content to life	What I plan to do	When will I do it?
1.		
2.		
3.		

Chapter Recap:

1. When crafting your content, use a logical sequence of information for better flow. But stay flexible, and consider which sequence will be most appealing to your audience.
2. Carefully consider the proper level of detail. What is the time frame? Who is your audience? Try to provide just enough detail to make your case, and no more.
3. Engage your audience, and bring content to life using stories, examples, anecdotes, and humor. Even technical presentations can benefit by a touch of lightness.

Chapter 3: Open and Close for Impact

Joanne was a bright young entrepreneur. After founding her business of advising other small firms about online marketing, she went on the speaking circuit in order to build visibility for her new venture. She was asked to speak to a women's group in her industry one evening. The attendees were very relaxed after drinks and dinner when she got there. Needless to say, she wasn't. Neither was the young woman who introduced her because first she forgot her own name; then she forgot Joanne's. When she finally stood up to speak, Joanne's first words were "Good morning. I mean good afternoon. I mean good evening." An inauspicious beginning if ever there was one.

When we began working together, Joanne was clear about one thing: she wanted to create better openings. Together we built a strategy for her in which she created her content first, and then went back to create a powerful opening, one that captured attention and made a connection with her audience. Since then, Joanne devotes a good portion of her preparation time to her opening, and she always rehearses it out loud.

Joanne is not alone. For many of us, the most challenging part of any presentation is the first minute or two. That is the time when we feel most vulnerable, most nervous, and most unfocused. It is also the time when your audience is forming its first impression of you and your expertise. No pressure, right?

However, with a little strategy, planning, and practice, you can capitalize on your openings to capture your audience's attention, build your confidence, and start your presentation with punch. Here are some suggestions.

Seven strategies to open your presentations with punch, pizzazz, and power

1. **Make your openings brief and positive.** If you want to have an impactful opening, move quickly into the heart of your presentation. Make your opening remarks brief and tie them directly to your Targeted Message. You can add background and context once you have set the stage.

2. **Talk about the audience and their concerns.** While it is important to establish your credibility with an audience, most times they are more impressed and engaged when you begin by speaking about what is most on their minds. You can work in your own qualifications as you go, or provide your credentials in the printed handout so those who wish can read it.

3. **Encourage audience interaction whenever appropriate.** You could start with something as simple as a question and show of hands, or have the audience greet their tablemates. These techniques take a lot of pressure off you, while allowing you to observe audience members, and see how they interact. Make sure that whatever interaction you plan to use does not eat up too much of your time or distract from the purpose of your presentation.

4. **Give your audience reasons to listen.** Remember the WIIFM (What's in it for me?), and stress it. Your audience wants to know what they need to do, or how they will be affected, or how they might benefit. By

putting your focus on what they want, you will find you are in tune almost instantly.

5. **Never apologize in your opening.** The room might be too crowded, too hot, or you might have technical problems at the beginning. Dig deep for a little humor, and don't let it throw you. Don't apologize for your slides, or the time of day. Don't tell them you are not an expert, or your slides are too busy, or you are not the most gifted speaker. Keep the focus on the quality of the information you are sharing with them.

6. **Use a "Power of Three" Opening.** This means you use three questions, or three statements, or three images to set the pace, and to focus your audience's attention on your message. You can also use three facts, but make them impressive, or three stories or vignettes, but make them brief. The whole greeting and opening should not last more than one to two minutes. Then tie it to your Targeted Message.

7. **Rehearse your opening out loud until you feel fully confident.** Rehearsing in your head is not as reliable as rehearsing out loud. You may know your material cold, and trust yourself to be able to speak without a full rehearsal, but *never trust* your opening in the same way. It is difficult to overcome a negative first impression, and then to get back on track if you derail. Take time to say your opening out loud at least three times, so you are sure you will be able to open without looking at your notes.

> **"** Listeners form a first impression in seconds. Make sure your openings create a positive impression and build rapport with your audience.

Once you have built a great message and mapped out your content, you are ready to prepare your opening. You will save time and worry by using the Power of Three to create an opening because it's fast, easy, and reliable.

Why three? Three seems to be a special number, and you will often see sets of three in advertisements, jokes, and literature. Think about nursery rhymes, children's stories, poems—very often there are three characters, or three actions taken by a character. You can take advantage of this natural cadence to create a series of three questions, three statements, or three words, moving your audience toward your Targeted Message, and launching your presentation with power.

Create your opening from your audience's point of view, stressing their concerns. Make sure you hit the right tone, which could be anything from humorous to strictly business. It depends on the situation, and the emotions of the audience, as well as how you want to move and impact them.

"Power of Three" Openings

Use parallel structure, that is, start each opening line with the same or similar words. Parallel structure makes it easier for you to remember the next line, and creates a cadence, similar to telling a joke or a story. It also builds anticipation in your audience's mind.

Keep your sentences or phrases simple, and experiment until your opening flows well, and is easy for you to remember.

Make sure you can tie it to your Targeted Message.

Here are a few ideas to jump-start your opening. Remember your opening can set the tone, remind people of something they know, arouse their curiosity, or acknowledge their feelings. Consider being a little bit provocative or humorous when it is appropriate.

"Power of Three" Opening Starters

Here are some ideas about how to build the cadence of the power of three. Use one of these as a jumping off point to create your own opening for your Targeted Message.

Structure	Example
3 Questions	What is a mass spectrometer? Why do we use it? How do we use it?
Targeted Message	Today as I answer those questions you will see exactly how the mass spectrometer helps us identify the amount and type of chemicals present in a sample.
Timeline	Ten years ago we were struggling to bring in enough business to stay afloat. That was a tough time. Five years ago we brought in our first sales manager and started hiring experienced reps. Things began to look a bit better then. Over the past year and a half, we have surpassed all sales projections, and built a solid base of happy and loyal customers. This has been a positive and exciting time for all of us.
Targeted Message	Today we know that in order to continue growing our business, we will need to upgrade our Customer Management Systems.
3 Statements	We have had many conversations about the need for new lab equipment. Some of you have said, "Wait until we move to the new plant."

	Some of you have said, "Purchase new equipment even though we are moving into our new plant next year."
	Some have even said, "Why do we need to do anything? Let's stick with our current equipment and save our money."
Targeted Message	The purpose of this presentation is to show you that the best course of action is to upgrade our lab equipment now, which will save money in the short term, while allowing us to postpone purchasing new until we move to the new plant.
3 Questions with engagement	Let's see a show of hands: How many of you are have a LinkedIn profile? How many of you are on Facebook? How many are on Twitter?
Targeted Message	Today you are going to see that in order to connect with our customers and build trusting relationships with them we need to create and distribute meaningful content through social media.

Build your own "Power of Three" Opening

Take a moment to think about the Targeted Message you have created. What is your audience thinking or feeling as they hear it? What do you want them to feel or think?

Draft an opening for your message using only three lines. Practice saying it out loud once or twice. See how it flows. If you aren't quite satisfied, edit, and repeat until you love it.

Opening Line 1:

Opening Line 2:

Opening Line 3:

Targeted Message:

Rehearse your opening out loud, being sure it has cadence and impact, and connects audience concerns directly to your Targeted Message.

Susan's presentation was going well, and she was feeling terrific. She had opened with a series of three compelling questions, and then clearly stated her Targeted Message. She had gone on to support her message with just the right level of detail. She was well-rehearsed, and she felt focused and calm. She took a few questions, and answered them well. As she came to the close of her presentation, she knew her timing was right on. She breathed a sigh of relief, and then abruptly stated, "Well, that's about all I have today. Thank you for coming."

What just happened? Susan had forgotten one of the most important parts of the presentation: her close. Susan and I started our coaching session soon after this presentation, and we began by discussing the importance of the closing. A weak closing feels incomplete and lacks punch. A stronger closing drives home your message or call to action, and leaves the audience feeling satisfied. Today, Susan plans her closing and rehearses it before each presentation. She won't get caught flat-footed again.

It's natural to run out of steam at the end of your presentation. But don't let the same thing happen to you.

> " Plan and rehearse your ending so you can end on a positive, memorable note.

Closing with impact

Because people tend to remember what they hear first, and what they hear last, your closing is a key component to your successful presentation. You will want to quickly summarize what you said, appropriately express appreciation, and most important, restate your Targeted Message or call to action. After all, this is what you want people to remember, or the action you want them to take. You can seal the deal with a good close.

But great closings don't happen spontaneously. With good planning, you can create a bit of anticipation—and end with a bang. Some strategies include:

- Remind people what they have learned or accomplished by listening to you.
- Thank them, not for their time, but for their participation, feedback, or comments.
- Be careful not to use the words "in closing" or "in conclusion" until you are ready to end.
- If you want more questions, ask, "What questions do you have?"
- A brisk "Thank you" will create closure after a long question-and-answer period.
- Try to close after a positive question, or on a positive note.
- Always end with a reminder of your Targeted Message, perhaps adding a brief call to action.

Ways to make your closing memorable

If your presentation is formal, or you are ending a conference or training session where people have been together for some time, you will find it makes sense to invest a bit more time in creating a memorable closing. You might include music, movement, special words, or a brief ceremony. Think it through to choose the most appropriate ending, watch your time, and select something with which you feel comfortable.

Suggestions:

1. A story with a happy ending
2. A future scenario
3. A reminder of the benefits they will enjoy
4. A humorous look at the content
5. Action plans or next steps
6. A cartoon
7. A song
8. A beautiful illustration or photo
9. A rallying cry, cheer, or chant performed by all
10. A simple ceremony, for example, having everyone stand up and shake hands with one another
11. A chance for audience members to speak to one another
12. A round of applause for the audience members and their great work

Create your closing

Think about the presentation you are working on. What do you want your audience to remember or do at the end of this presentation?

Take a moment to select a strategy or two from the lists above. In the space below, draft your closing, ending with your Targeted Message.

Say it out loud. Does it sound strong and decisive? If not, rewrite until it does.

Chapter Recap:

1. Openings are key for setting the stage, engaging the audience, and putting you in a confident position. Take time to plan and rehearse your openings.
2. Structure can be helpful to ensure consistent openings. Consider the Power of Three: three questions, three statements, or three facts, followed by your Targeted Message. This creates a cadence of forward momentum.
3. Closings are too important to leave to chance. Thoroughly plan and rehearse your closings as well as openings.

Chapter 4: Rehearse for Success

Chris was getting ready for a major presentation in which he would be speaking to the board of his organization. They had asked him to give an update on his project. His intention was to spend time putting his thoughts together so he would be well prepared. At first he wasn't sure what they were looking for, so he sent a quick email to his boss asking for clarification. Then he went on to his next meeting, and his next and his next.

Days passed, and suddenly it was the day before the presentation, and Chris was not ready. In a panic, Chris spent the final day working on his presentation while sitting in on conference calls, half listening and half focusing on his presentation. His frustration mounted as the day continued. There was no way he would have time to rehearse. As a result, his presentation was fragmented, and he felt frazzled and out of control.

How important is rehearsal to you?

Maybe you aren't talking with the board, but instead you are giving a more routine presentation. It might not seem like a big deal—unless you are new in your role, and you need to make a great first impression on your new team. Or you are giving a sales presentation to win a major new account, or to keep one you are in danger of losing. Or maybe the public's impression of your firm is at stake. Even "routine" presentations are often important enough to rehearse.

> *You will always present more confidently and successfully if you have rehearsed properly.*

When deciding how much time to invest, ask yourself the following:

How formal is it?

If it's a few words at the company picnic, you might decide that rehearsing is not critically important. But when it's a media presentation, or a chance to pitch your ideas to the board, then you will want to be thoroughly prepared and well-rehearsed.

How familiar are you with the content?

If you have spoken frequently on the same topic, you might only need do a quick rehearsal or review to be ready. But when the content is complex, controversial, or new to you, it pays for you to spend more time preparing and rehearsing so you sound polished and confident.

Now, take a look at the following types of rehearsals, and select the one or two you think will be appropriate and most effective in making you feel comfortable and confident about your material.

As you go. As you create each part of your presentation (Targeted Message, Opening, Closing, slides), speak each one out loud. You will see how the content flows, and how it sounds as you speak it. *Bonus:* you are rehearsing even as you are testing and refining it.

Timed rehearsal. This can also be done at any time as you develop each slide, or as you develop sections of a longer presentation. You may time your presentation with a stopwatch, or by using the timed-rehearsal function in PowerPoint. *Bonus:* you can adjust the timing as you go, instead of waiting for the final rehearsal.

Without visuals. Try rehearsing your presentation without notes or visuals. You'll discover how well you know the content, and you'll also get a sense of how it flows. You will see where you need to add depth with a case study, details, additional facts, or an illustrative story. You are learning and refining the content without relying on visuals, which means your final delivery will be smoother.

With visuals. Try viewing your slides in Notes view, then type your script or notes on the bottom half of each page. Or print out the slide view, and handwrite your notes on the bottom of each printed page. Now you can take your slides with you wherever you go, and practice one slide, one section, or the whole thing from beginning to end.

Recorded. Using video or audio recording, you will be able to "see and hear" yourself as your audience does. How well do you enunciate and use vocal inflections and variety? How many filler words like "um" are you using? Do you sound engaged? What is the recorded time?

With a test audience. You can't beat having people listen to your actual presentation. Do more than simply tell them about the presentation; deliver it just as you will to your real audience. Be sure to ask for specific feedback. You might also ask them to pepper you with tough questions they think might arise. Make sure to adjust as needed, then check your timing again.

Full-dress. Full-dress rehearsal means giving the entire presentation from beginning to end, with all the slides, activities, discussion, and Q&A. You could record this one if you have not done so already. You could have your test audience attend again, especially if you have made major changes, based on their feedback. Check your time; by now it should be right where you want it. Adjust the opening and closing as needed for maximum impact.

Here are additional strategies to maximize your success.

Once you have created and fully rehearsed your presentation, take time to celebrate. For those of you who tend to underprepare, you should feel proud of yourself for being so organized. And those of you who over-prepare (and you know who you are), you can relax, knowing that you are ready. Take time to revisit your confidence-building strategies and affirmations to remind yourself how great you are, and how well the presentation is going to go.

Three or four days ahead of your presentation, check the slides, links, and visuals. It's a final review, as well as a mini-rehearsal. If you have loaded the presentation onto a flash drive or a laptop, it's important to ensure that all the links work, and everything is good to go. If you need to use internet connections during your presentation, make sure you will have easy access. Either stop by the presentation space to check it out, or ask for a technician to be there as you set up. Please don't assume everything will work, especially if your presentation relies on technology.

If you don't already have one, get a remote slide advancer so you can run the presentation without being glued to the computer. Most remote slide advancers will start and end your slideshow, give you a black or white screen, and advance or reverse the slides. It goes without saying, learn which buttons do what, and try it out so you know how long it takes the slide to advance. Some remotes have a laser pointer, and some have silent timers, which is a nice thing to have right in your hand. Bring a few extra batteries, or put a fresh one in so you know you have full power.

On the day of your presentation be sure to get there early. You will want to leave a little extra time for traffic, or getting past security, or anything else that could slow you down. Once you arrive, set up your equipment, load your presentation, and check the chairs, lighting, and temperature. Move around the room, getting comfortable with the space. Go up and down the steps to the lectern, if you are using one. Do a quick sound check if you are using a microphone. Use the restroom, and check your teeth and clothing, to be sure your image is exactly how you want it to be.

Final reminders

- Calm yourself. If you feel a bit of last-minute jitters, don't panic. Take slow, deep breaths, and remind yourself that you are fully prepared and ready to go.

- Meet and greet. Once you are in the room, and all is ready, welcome people as they arrive. You may not be a master of small talk, but you don't need to be. Ask a question or two, and listen to the answers. Connect with your audience, and put them at ease. It takes much of the pressure off you.

- Smile, you're on. Be sure to smile as you move into the front of the room. Keep breathing, and make eye contact with those who came to hear you. It is your moment, and you are thoroughly prepared. It is your time to shine.

Reflection for Rehearsal

1. How has a lack of rehearsal impacted you in the past?

2. What would be an ideal level of rehearsal for you?

3. How can you dedicate the time and focus you need to rehearse for success?

Chapter Recap:

1. For most of us, finding time and energy for rehearsal is a challenge, though it generally results in a more polished presentation. Decide how much rehearsal you will need for each different situation, and then make time for it. If your presentation is important, preparing fully is a must.
2. Look for ways to incorporate rehearsal as you go so that you make the most of your time.
3. Consider recording your rehearsals, or presenting in front of a test audience. Each of these provides you with valuable feedback.
4. If time is short, focus on the parts of the presentation that need the most rehearsal; the beginning, the end, and maybe a few spots in the middle that require fine-tuning.

Chapter 5: Be Brilliant with Visuals

Jacob, a brilliant strategist in a new cutting-edge technology firm, was giving his first presentation in front of prospective investors. He stood glued to his slides projected on the screen—and for more than ten minutes, he spoke without once glancing toward his audience. His message was good, his content was fine, but his delivery was not working. Later he admitted he knew he had turned to the screen too much, but he couldn't seem to break the habit.

As we worked on his upcoming presentations, I suggested he keep his feet pointed toward his audience so he never turned away from them completely. He was soon able to glance at the screen and then return his attention to his audience. Result: instant credibility.

Sadly, Jacob isn't the only person who struggles with visual aids. In fact, this happens way too often. Some of the most brilliant, funny speakers go lifeless the moment they turn on their crowded, content-bloated slides. But it doesn't have to be that way.

> " For visual appeal and increased retention, move away from masses of bullets and dense content, and toward more streamlined, visually compelling slides.

If you frequently present with slides, I encourage you to take a fresh look at both your slide design and your slide delivery. We will start with slide delivery tips, and then observe key principles for effective slide design.

While I sincerely hope you will experiment with more attractive and compelling slides, if your organization or boss wants the visuals to follow a certain format, you would be smart to stay within those boundaries. Even so, there are subtle but powerful changes you might be able to work into your next presentation.

To deliver brilliantly with slides:

Get a clicker, and use it to start, end, and click through your slides. No more asking someone else to turn each slide, or bending over to reach the keyboard. This makes it easier on you, while keeping the focus on your message.

Look at your laptop, not the screen. Never turn your back to your audience, because once you do, you'll end up looking at the screen more than your audience. If you must point to something on the screen, keep your feet and shoulders facing forward, and point to the side. This way you can easily turn back to the audience.

Interpret slides, rather than reading them. Nothing is more boring than a speaker who reads what is on each slide. We know this, and yet sometimes we do it. Put fewer words on each slide. Use key words instead of sentences. Interpret what the content means. Add something interesting to what is on each slide. Tell a story about the content, or have a conversation about it. Whatever you do, just don't read it line by line.

Don't comment on every point on the slides. Sometimes a high-level discussion is fine. Pick out the pertinent items, and elaborate on them. Pull out key facts or highlights. Provide an anecdote or illustration that ties the content together.

Break away from the slides. Start a discussion, get into an impromptu Q&A session, or blacken the screen, and then talk directly to the audience. This is fresh and unexpected. (Maybe you don't even need all those slides.)

Show real people and faces. Show your team, your colleagues who couldn't be there, or even your own photo for a virtual presentation. Faces of people from your organization or industry always trump canned stock photos.

Be radical: present without slides. Or use only a few. This is not the norm in most organizations today, but it is refreshing when people move away from slides, and focus on the audience and the message. If this seems too extreme for your organization, prepare as usual, but start by using fewer slides, keeping the rest on reserve.

Key principals for brilliant slide design

Sometimes even minor changes will make your visuals work so much better. Check out your next presentation, and see if you can put these tips below to work:

Add an opening and closing slide. These can have your presentation's title, your name, your company, the date, or an image. Don't have data on the first or last slide. At these critical points you want your audience's attention on you, not what is on the slides.

Do some serious pruning. You may start out with long, wordy bullet points, extraneous text, and far too many slides. As you practice with the content, see what words, bullets, or slides can be streamlined, hidden or eliminated.

Search out any unnecessary words, paragraphs, diagrams, or other elements you can live without. You may like them because you think they look "cool," but "less is more." Does it really add value? If not, leave it out.

Be comfortable with white space. Visually, if the slide is too "full," no one will want to read it. And if it is too full, you are more likely to read it. Not good. Put less on each slide, or break your content into more slides. Consider using a "build effect" if your slide has many elements.

Remove unnecessary bullets. You don't need to bullet everything. You can omit bullets and use bolding of key words or paragraph markers, especially when you have three or fewer items. And if you only have one item, why put a bullet in front of it? Skip it.

Remove punctuation. Bullet points by definition are not sentences, so most of the time you can simply leave off the punctuation. If you see that you are using complete sentences, see if you can reduce them to key words. And watch for inconsistent punctuation; it drives some people crazy.

Remove boxes. Many times we place boxes around headlines, call outs and other elements for no apparent reason. Skip them unless you really need to use them for clarity. If you need to highlight an element with a box, consider a softly colored one without edges. And if it is a "bumper sticker" meant as a final word or reminder, consider bringing it in at the end as a build.

Don't use all caps. Sometimes people use all caps on headlines, or to highlight key words. This is unattractive, and often is considered "shouting." Use bolding if you need to highlight certain words. Or choose a different font, size or color. You may also italicize a few key words or phrases.

Don't underline words. Save underlining for hyperlinks, since this is what people expect when they see something underlined. Why not highlight important information with size, italics, or bolding?

Vary headlines. Don't use the same headline on each visual throughout your presentation. It will lose all meaning, and it simply wastes space. It's more effective to use headlines to tell your story, or to separate different segments of the presentation.

Skip templates. Avoid canned templates, especially those with dark backgrounds, unless you are asked to use a standard corporate template. Dark or black text on a white background is generally crisp and clear, and easy to see even when the room is bright.

Avoid decorative elements such as Clip Art, WordArt, fancy effects and transitions. Unless you are very skilled at making them an integral part of the design, they can look amateurish. Just keep it simple, or leave them out.

Don't animate text from the bottom up, or from right to left. Rule: text should appear from left to right, or top to bottom, which is how we read. You can be safer using simple transitions, such as "appear" and "fade in." It is fine to use "builds" occasionally, but don't call attention to the transitions, only the content.

Use photos, not clip art. Don't use tiny pictures. Enlarge them so that they fill a quarter to a third of the slide, or fill the screen entirely. Use photos of your company, your team, or pictures that suggest a mood or tone that might help people remember what you said. Don't use clip art; it almost always looks dated and amateurish.

Take your own photos and videos. They are unique, and royalty-free, plus you don't have to worry about copyright permission. Your photos must be fairly high quality and interesting. Consider photos of a customer using your product, or your plant or shop floor. Check with your organization to see if you need permission to use these photos.

Watch for typos. Remember if you use the wrong word, but spell it correctly, the spell-checker won't correct it. It's often easier to spot these little errors if you print a hard copy of your slides or notes pages. Better yet, ask someone to proof your presentation.

Consider hyperlinking. Don't pack everything onto the slide, but add hyperlinks to spreadsheets, videos, websites, etc. Your slides should be easier to read this way, and less cluttered. Also note:

- If you import your presentation containing hyperlinks to a jump drive, your links will be broken. Always check to make sure the links are working.
- If you send your slides to someone else, the linked content won't automatically be included.
- Linked information won't appear on your printed speaker notes or handout pages.

Use Notes Pages for text. Ideally, your slideshow won't look like a script, but it should be a visual complement to what you are saying. If you think you might need a prompt, type your "script" in Notes view, then print it out for practice, and use it as a script for the presentation if you need it. (It also makes a great backup if technology fails.)

Rehearse! Practice your content out loud several times, working with your slides. Don't read what's onscreen only in your head, but actually say those words out loud until you feel the flow. Chances are if you prepare in this way, you will be able to present from the slides, and won't need the notes.

Take advantage of brilliant shortcuts. There are a number of very useful and cool shortcuts you can perform while in slideshow view. You can blacken your screen, jump to a different slide, start a hyperlinked action like a video, or show a hidden slide.

Think about what you want to do, then find the corresponding short cut. Practice this until you can perform it easily, or create a "cheat sheet" by putting several shortcuts on a sticky note. Here are just a few of the most useful shortcuts:

Action desired:	Key:
Start a presentation from the beginning	F5
Perform the next animation or advance to the next slide	N, ENTER, PAGE DOWN, RIGHT ARROW, DOWN ARROW, or SPACEBAR
Perform the previous animation or return to the previous slide	P, PAGE UP, LEFT ARROW, UP ARROW, or BACKSPACE
Go to a specific slide number	Desired Slide Number + ENTER
Display a blank black slide, or return to the presentation from a blank black slide	B or PERIOD
Display a blank white slide, or return to the presentation from a blank white slide	W or COMMA
End a presentation	ESC or HYPHEN
Erase on-screen annotations	E

Go to the next slide, if the next slide is hidden	**H**
Return to the first slide	**A** or **=**
Change the pointer to a pen	**CTRL+P**
Change the pointer to an arrow	**CTRL+A**
Hide the pointer and navigation button immediately	**CTRL+H**
View the computer taskbar	**CTRL+T**

To use the special functions of PowerPoint, you need to stay in "slide show" view. Once you exit slide show, you can no longer use any of these special functions, and the audience can see your desktop, which shows all your icons and projects. It is better for them to see your final slide, a repeat of your title slide, or even a blank slide.

Practice:

Select one to three of the shortcuts shown on the chart above. Open a PowerPoint presentation, enter Slideshow view, and try them. If you use a different slide program, find and practice similar shortcuts.

Question: which ones will you use during your next presentation?

Chapter Recap:

1. Slide design is critical to ensure that slides are attractive, appealing, and easy to read.
2. Well-designed slides help your listeners—as well as you—to stay focused on what is most important.
3. Master the art of delivering skillfully from slides, and not reading them, or relying on them as a crutch. To make this happen, rehearse often with your slides.
4. Learn a few shortcuts so you can move even more efficiently through your slides as needed.

Chapter 6: Engage and Respond

Mary was a brilliant sales manager. She was great when speaking with clients, on the phone, or in person. Quick on her feet, Mary was able to draw out her listener by asking good questions, and could answer questions and challenges with ease. But when she was put in front of a larger audience, she froze. Her mind went blank, and she lost her focus. As a result, she rushed through her presentation in order to quickly wrap it up. Her audience was left feeling surprised and disappointed.

During our coaching sessions, Mary expressed frustration about not being better in front of large groups. She was beginning to lose confidence. Instead struggling to be someone she wasn't, we hit upon the idea of building on her strengths by turning her large-group presentations into conversations. With a few minor modifications, Mary learned to use her powerful engagement skills to turn dry presentations into lively conversations. What a difference that made!

Have you ever felt like Mary? What a shame, because you probably could have had an engaging conversation with your audience—and they would probably have loved it.

Today's skilled speakers tend to be concerned about their audiences as much as with the content they wish to share. They consider an audience's concerns and hot buttons. They determine what information the audience needs, and think about how they might prefer to receive it. They plan on ways to keep audience members engaged and interested.

I think this shift toward audience-focus is great for the audience, as well as for you, the speaker. But it definitely adds another element to speaking, which means using a different skillset.

> " The best presentations strike a fine balance between content, delivery, and engagement.

Is it worth it? Many of my clients say that once they make the connection with their audiences, they forget about self-consciousness and enjoy being in the present moment.

However you choose to do it, I encourage you to reach out and connect with your audience. Decide which of the strategies below might be most suitable for you and your audience, and give them a try.

Prepare your content with the audience in mind. Why do they need to hear this? What do they need to do about it? How will it impact them? Keeping these questions in mind will help you to create content that is intrinsically more interesting to the audience.

Ask questions of the audience. "How are you today? What brings you here? What is on your mind?" Be sincere in asking, and listen thoughtfully to the responses. This dialogue will help you adapt your content appropriately, and might affect the examples and stories you share.

Plan an interactive opening. Consider breaking a large group into smaller groups, and then move around to listen to what they have to say. Or ask them to state their concerns, or write them on cards or on a flip chart.

Be there now. In order to engage, you have to be fully present, not distracted by your own agenda or script. With a little practice, you will find it easier to foster and engage in a discussion during your presentations instead of just telling.

> 66 Start with easy questions that make it easy for people to interact with you, then work toward more complex issues.

Build your question-asking skills. Asking the right questions at the right time doesn't always come automatically. Plan the questions you might want to ask, but keep an open mind. You will need to adjust your questions depending on the responses you get back. You can start by learning about the three types of questions and when to use them.

Closed Ended Questions

Many of us find it easy to use closed-ended questions, and because they are easy we tend to rely on them too much. "Are you with me?" "Follow me?" "Any questions so far?" Note that each of these questions can be answered with a simple yes or no, and sometimes that is all you need. When you want a quick pulse-check, closed-ended questions do the job. They are often easy for the audience to answer, so they are good ones to start with. Not all closed-ended questions are easy though, so it's best to start with questions that are non-threatening and non-revealing.

Questions like these should be easy for the audience to respond to:

"How many of you have become lost on your way to a client meeting? Let's see a show of hands."

"Have you noticed that most meetings start late? Or is it just my meetings?"

"Have you ever been nervous about an important presentation? I know I have."

Then move to questions that are more difficult to respond to. Questions like these are definitely thought-provoking, and participants might be uncomfortable answering them publicly:

"How many of you have ever texted while driving?"

"How many of you have ever cheated on your expense report?"

"Have you ever told a lie to save face?"

You might use difficult closed-ended questions like these rhetorically to make your audience members think. But don't expect a huge response until *after* you have built a high degree of trust with your audience. The general rule is to start with the most benign questions, then gradually move toward more challenging ones.

But closed-ended questions only go so far. If you keep using them over and over, it will seem like you are quizzing the listeners, and your discussion won't go very deep. When you need to gather more information, or elicit more answers, you will want to move to open-ended questions.

Open-ended questions

Open-ended questions require more than a yes or no answer. With open-ended questions you are seeking more information or more ideas. For example, they might result in a list of benefits, or options, or recommendations. Like closed-ended questions, they can be relatively easy to answer, or more challenging.

Questions like these should be fairly easy for most audiences to answer:

"What do you think is the most common type of operator error?"

"Without naming names, what safety rules get broken most often?"

"Who has a different take on this?"

But questions like these will be more difficult for a typical audience to answer

"What can we do as leaders to improve employee satisfaction scores?"

"What would you do if you saw someone breaking a safety rule?"

"Under what circumstances might a lie be morally justifiable?"

Probing questions

Probing questions ask listeners to dig deeper into reasons, opinions, ramifications, or results. You might find these questions more difficult to ask, but with a little practice, you can probe skillfully until you have the rich, deep information you want.

> *To ask probing questions, listen to the answers to questions already asked, then use your next questions to dig deeper.*

Because you are asking questions based on previous answers, it might be difficult to preplan the exact probing questions to use. However, you might think ahead about which probing questions might be asked, and then be willing to adjust on the fly.

Questions like these might work well to probe deeper:

"Why do you think these safety rules need to be reviewed every year?"

"What might happen if we let engagement scores slip further?"

"What else could you have done to resolve that customer issue?"

Getting the discussion going

Planning and asking great questions is a good start. But how can you be sure you can get a discussion rolling? Here are some strategies that can be useful to prepare the right conditions for an interactive presentation or discussion.

Interact early and often. Many times I see speakers who deliver their entire presentation, and only at the end do they ask for comments or reaction. Often by then, it is way too late. Worse, sometimes people will say, *"I welcome your questions as we go; I want this to be interactive."* But then they start talking, and never stop for a question or reaction.

If you truly want interaction, don't tell the audience you want interaction, simply start that way. You can use a show of hands in your introduction; *"How many of you have experienced flight delays and the frustrations that go with them? I thought so. Well, our customers experience the same frustrations when our products are delayed, and today we are going to explore ways to streamline production. Let's start out by teaming up and discussing this issue with the person sitting next to you. What can we do to speed production? In two minutes I will ask you what you discussed."*

With this interactive opening, you have made it easy for your audience to engage. You have used emotions to engage them in feeling like the customer feels. You have also clearly signaled that this is going to be more than a sit-and-listen presentation, without having to say so.

> " If you don't get an immediate response from the audience, try asking them to discuss their answers with the person sitting closest to them.

Start with table discussions. Once they start talking to each other, you can observe their reactions. Do they have a lot to say to each other, or does the discussion quickly fizzle out? Do you see facial animation and gestures? If so, they are willing to engage, but need a warm-up like the small-group discussion.

Give them a few minutes to talk, and then ask them about their ideas. Get a couple of answers from around the room. The next time you ask a question, you may get a faster response. If not, go back to table discussions. Many groups find it easier speaking with one other person or at tables rather than speaking up in front of the large group.

You might repeat this process a few times before they become more comfortable with sharing in the large group, or you might decide to stick with the small group discussions, enhanced with a large-group debrief.

Give them time. Whenever you ask a question, stop a moment and wait for the response. Sometimes if a group is uncomfortable, or is unsure what you are asking, they need a moment to process. Don't jump in to ask the question a different way, or they will be more confused. If you wait a moment or two, and nothing happens, you could repeat the question, and then wait. If no one answers, you could look around to see if anyone is making eye contact with you. If so, you could try calling on that person. Generally, don't call on someone who is not willing to make eye contact with you; they are not ready or don't want to be put on the spot.

Loosen up and share control. As a presenter, you may have learned that you need to master every detail, rehearse every word and gesture—and be in full control of yourself and the situation. If you plan to engage and interact with your audience, you will probably need to learn how to give up the control reins some of the time.

This can feel scary, because you don't have control over what your audience does or says. But it can also be exhilarating. Let the audience participate, and together you can create something wonderful. If you refuse to hear them out, they can become highly resistant, clam up, and disengage.

Interactive techniques to try:

- ☐ Ask for a show of hands
- ☐ Ask questions, and wait for the answers
- ☐ Have audience members introduce themselves, and say something about the subject matter
- ☐ Ask audience members to introduce themselves to one another in small groups
- ☐ Start with a small group or table discussion
- ☐ Give audience members a task to complete
- ☐ Provide a quiz or test, either orally or written
- ☐ Have audience members jot down their thoughts or questions
- ☐ Ask audience members to provide comments or examples
- ☐ Ask audience members to work on a case study
- ☐ Ask for volunteers to write on the flip chart
- ☐ Ask audience members to solve a problem

- ☐ Ask audience members to share their ideas or reactions
- ☐ Conduct brief icebreaker
- ☐ Have audience members write their concerns, thoughts or questions on sticky notes, and then post them on a wall
- ☐ If appropriate (for example, at a conference,) have audience members Tweet their comments or questions during your talk
- ☐ Have audience members teach each other some of the content

Responding to Questions

Jill was worried. As part of a regional planning organization, she and her team were preparing for a series of community meetings in which local residents would be able to comment on the proposal now underway. It was important to hear community input, but everyone was not going to be happy about the proposed changes. Jill was worried that her team members would freeze up when faced with angry outbursts or strong objections. She knew they were already nervous about it. How could she help prepare them—and herself—for difficult questions?

In the workshop we delivered, Jill and her team practiced on each other. They took turns asking and fielding the most difficult questions they could imagine. Each person had the chance to practice maintaining composure, restating the question with a bridge, and then answering the question. When the live presentation took place a few weeks later, everyone was able to confidently face and answer the tough questions that came up.

Can you handle the heat? How are you at answering questions that come up during your presentation?

- Are you light on your feet and quick with answers during a lively Q&A?
- Are you polished and confident when you are peppered with challenging or even hostile questions?
- Or do you feel more like the team in the example above?

> If answering the audience's questions makes you uncomfortable, rehearse with a pilot audience, having them ask you tough questions until you can field them with ease.

Interestingly, many people who are flustered or stiff during their presentations come alive during Q&A. And others who are comfortable and polished during their presentations may stumble when surprised or challenged.

Here's the good news: with a little practice and a few special techniques, we can all learn to rise to the occasion, think and respond more quickly, and become more at ease when responding to tough questions.

Predict questions

In order to be prepared for questions during your presentation, the first step is to predict which ones you might expect to receive. If you can't or don't predict them, you could be in for a few nasty surprises. However, if you can anticipate questions, you can prepare yourself ahead of time with answers and strategies for handling them like a pro.

The next time you prepare for a presentation, take time to list the questions you think might arise. Then ask someone who knows your content or your audience to add to your list.

Once you have listed the questions, ensure you have good answers for them, even if it means doing more research. Consider incorporating some of the answers into your presentation. This might circumvent some of the tough questions before they are even asked.

Encourage your audience to ask questions

What if no one asks you a single question? Maybe it's because they are stunned by your brilliance. Or maybe you covered everything to their satisfaction. But a few good questions can add life to even a technical presentation, so it makes sense to encourage your audience to ask. Here are some strategies that might make them more willing to engage.

Save time for Q&A. A great strategy is to allow enough time at the end for questions, rather than packing your presentation too full of information and using all your time. Next time try saving about 10-15 percent of your time for questions and answers. If you do happen to wrap up a few minutes sooner than scheduled, most audiences will be pleased, and a few people might stay behind to chat with you.

Take questions intermittently. Consider taking questions at intervals throughout your presentation. For example, when you finish one section, ask for questions about that content, and so on. In this way, you engage the audience earlier, and you get to hear what they are thinking before you move on to another topic.

Reinforce the behavior you want. Check to be sure you are responding positively to each question. If you respond with even mild sarcasm or dismissal, you will discourage further questions. To help keep it positive, you might respond to the first few questions with, "Thank you for the question."

Provide brief answers. Many speakers go on and on in their answers, which can discourage the audience from asking more. It can also lead to your presentation taking too much time, or going down "rabbit trails" of no interest to most of your audience. Enlist someone to give you feedback on how you respond. Do you ramble on and on, go off on tangents, or fail to get back on track? Practice with someone who can coach you to answer succinctly, and to move forward.

To maintain forward momentum after questions, avoid saying, *"Getting back to the presentation,"* or *"As I was saying."* It is better to move forward by using a phrase like *"next,"* or *"now,"* or *"moving on."* Why move backward when you can move forward?

Manage your time

If you tend toward long answers, get a stopwatch and practice answering what you consider typical questions. If your answers are longer than two or three minutes, practice tightening up your answers until you can provide responses to most questions in one or two minutes. If you find this difficult, ask someone to work with you, or record your answers, and then try them again, making the answer shorter and shorter.

> " During Q&A, keep your answers brief and factual rather than going into overly long or technical answers.

Too many questions?

Sometimes you get more questions than you wanted. In this case, stop thanking people for the questions, simply take them one at a time—answer them and move forward. If it looks like there will be a very large number of questions, consider asking people to write them down on cards, and then collect them. You can sort through the questions, group them by topic, and answer the ones you think are most relevant.

When you need to finish your presentation, and the questions keep coming, don't say, "No more questions." Instead, state, "One more question before we need to wrap up," or "I would like to honor your time by wrapping this up." Then offer to stay or meet with others who have additional questions.

Build skills and fluency

The best way to become skillful at responding to questions is to practice—a lot. Make this part of your regular preparation process. You can benefit from practicing on your own, but working with a live audience is even better. Ask your team to help you predict questions, prepare and rehearse your answers, and practice moving forward.

If you discover you tend to answer questions bluntly or too briefly, your challenge might be to flesh out your answers with a bit more depth, or to slightly soften your response.

Take our quiz to find out how well you respond to questions during your presentations.

A Quiz: Test your Q&A Skills	T/F
I generally save enough time for a good Q&A session at the end.	
I often take control by planting a kick-off question, or by stating, *"A question I am often asked is..."*	
In order to encourage questions, I generally ask, *"What questions do you have?"* rather than *"Do you have any questions?"*	
I always let the person with the question finish asking it, even when the question goes on and on. I try hard to not interrupt a questioner.	

If there is a question from an angry or abusive audience member, I don't pass the question back to them. Instead I try to answer the general concern they have raised.	
When a question calls for discussion, opinion, or multiple answers, I sometimes pass it back to the audience, as a way to tackle (but not to avoid), a tough issue.	
I try to keep my eye contact moving slowly around the room, including everyone, not only the person with the question, so that I can keep everyone engaged in the discussion.	
When I don't know the answer, I admit it, and offer to find out, or get help from the audience.	
I don't ask my audience to hold their questions, but if I must, I explain why, and offer to answer all questions at the end.	
I take a moment to think before I answer a question, and don't jump in too fast. I think this shows respect, and it also buys me time to think.	
Even when I am barraged with tough questions, I focus on breathing to control my emotions and my voice, and I try to keep a neutral facial expression.	
I avoid saying, *"That's a good question,"* or *"I'm glad you asked,"* since these phrases can sound	

sarcastic or insincere. I start by using neutral bridge, such as *"The question is about..."*	
When an emotionally charged or trigger word appears in the question, I substitute a neutral word, so that I don't repeat negative words or phrases.	
I don't let an angry or hostile questioner dominate the Q&A by asking, *"Who has another question?"* or *"Who has the next question?"*	

Dealing with difficult audiences

The best time to deal with a difficult or negative audience is in the preparation stage. If you predict that your audience might be hostile, you can preface your remarks with a neutral acknowledgment of their feelings: *"I understand there is a fair amount of concern about our new employee benefit plan, and I'm here today to answer all your questions..."* Note the word "concern," is used here, which is neutral, but still addresses the feelings.

If you are caught by surprise, stay calm, try to be reasonable without caving in, and if it seems appropriate, let people vent their feelings in a productive way before continuing.

Interruptions

Because interruptions can eat up your time, and may cause you to lose control of the situation, take action to minimize interruptions before they begin.

A good way to minimize interruptions is to ask for questions at the end of each segment. For example, *"Before I go on, what questions do you have about our new pricing strategy?"* In this way you receive questions in a logical sequence, and you create a more interactive presentation.

Bombarding questions

If you must ask your audience to hold their questions, give them a good reason, and make it clear that you are not avoiding questions. Try something like: *"Because of our extremely limited time frame for this meeting, I am going to ask you to allow me a few minutes to deliver a short statement. At the end I will take all your questions, and I will stay until I have answered every one."*

Hecklers

The most important guideline to follow when facing a heckler is to remain calm. It is almost impossible to win by arguing with a heckler, because even if you win the argument, you can lose the goodwill of the audience. In addition, if you lose your temper, you won't be able to think clearly.

When facing a heckler, try to stick to the issues, and remain factual but calm. Defend your position without becoming defensive. You may have to agree to disagree. Above all, do not agree with someone who is obviously wrong, just to keep the peace.

Remember, it's up to you to take control, but try to do so in a calm, professional manner. If you lose your temper, the heckler wins.

Highly emotional situations

If you feel yourself losing your cool, check out your body language. Have you clenched your fists, furrowed your brows, or crossed your arms across your chest? Your audience can see these signals. Relax your body, so that you appear calm. Take a few calming breaths, slowly and quietly.

Some speakers take a sip of water to buy a little time to calm down. Be honest about the situation, and offer a cool-down period or break if necessary.

Challenges and hostile questions

Does the thought of a hostile or challenging question make your blood run cold? Worried that you might not be able to stay calm? Think quickly? Provide a coherent answer?

> " When you receive a difficult or challenging question, listen carefully, remain calm, and answer it patiently and honestly.

Follow this approach to maintain focus and composure, respond to the question, and get back on track faster.

How to Handle Hostile Questions	
Stop, look, and listen	You cannot answer the question successfully unless you hear it. You show respect when you take the time to calmly listen, making eye contact with the person who asked the question, or who interrupted you.
Stay neutral	Don't cross your arms, frown, or roll your eyes. Try to show no reaction or emotion

	while considering the question—and your answer. Cultivate a calm, neutral demeanor.
Breathe	Remind yourself to breathe to bring oxygen to your brain, and to release tension. Take a quiet breath or two, but don't sigh.
Bridge	The Neutral Bridge is a verbal transition between the question and your answer. A neutral bridge buys you time to think, helps people in the audience who may not have heard the question, and demonstrates that you have understood the question.
Answer	Answer questions directly, briefly, and honestly. If you don't know the answer, admit it. You will lose credibility if you make up an answer or change the subject—so be straightforward. While answering, slowly move your eye contact around the room, looking at one person at a time, including the person who asked the question, but not exclusively at them.
Move forward	When you have answered the question, move ahead to your next point. Avoid saying, *"As I was saying"* by substituting, *"Next, let's turn our attention to…"* or *"The next topic on our agenda is…"*

Sample Neutral Bridges™

Try starting with these or similar Neutral Bridges™ to reframe or restate the question before answering it. For example, if someone has a question about what she describes as your "high prices," you might address "pricing," or the "value of your pricing." Use a Neutral Bridge™ like, *"The question is about the value our product brings to the market,"* or *"The question is about our pricing strategy."* You don't need to repeat the negative words contained in the question.

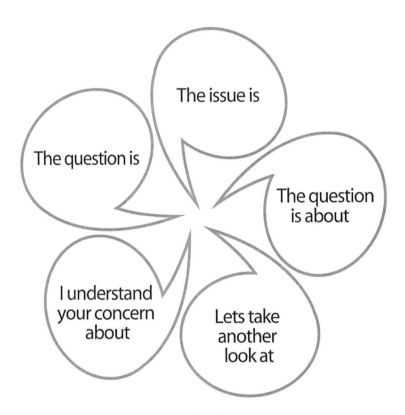

Practice makes for perfect Q&A

Prepare for your next presentation by brain-storming all the questions you could be asked, then prepare a Neutral

Bridge™ and an answer for each question. Ask someone to drill you until you can bridge and answer with ease.

Challenging Question	Neutral Bridge™	Answer

Chapter Recap:

1. Prepare your presentation for interaction by developing it *with the audience in mind*. Tailor your message and content specifically to their interests and needs.
2. Encourage interaction by being open, welcoming, and curious about what your audience thinks. Be sure your face and body language are open, not closed.
3. Use a variety of engagement techniques, geared toward making it easy and nonthreatening for listeners to engage and respond.
4. Use questions to help the audience open up to you. Start with easy to answer questions before moving to probing or sensitive questions.
5. Listen carefully to questions, then rephrase with a Neutral Bridge™ before answering.
6. Don't get stuck answering questions from one or two audience members: engage the entire audience in the question and answer session.

Chapter 7: Turn Nerves to Power

Is fear holding you back?

Marci was a new manager in the audit department of a large accounting firm. For most of her career she had managed to stay behind the scenes, working on client issues, and reporting back to her supervisor, who handled most of the client contact. Now as a new leader, she knew she had to begin speaking in front of clients, partners of her firm, and larger audiences at accounting conferences. Marci knew she had to get over the nerves—or it was going to make this new role difficult and painful.

Luckily, Marci was determined to step up and get past her nerves. We worked on her internal dialog and changed her self-critical thinking to positive, nurturing self-talk. She learned to stand in a calm, grounded way, and to breathe to ease her nervousness. Later, she saw herself on video and exclaimed, "I don't even look nervous anymore!"

For many people, dealing with nervousness is real and painful. It gets in the way of communicating effectively. It keeps them hiding in the dark when they should be shining. If this sounds familiar, this chapter is definitely for you.

What is this fear all about? I'm sure we aren't born with nervousness. Think of the two- or three-year-olds you know. Most of them I know are willing to sing or dance or speak in front of anyone. But then something happens. They forget their lines, or make a mistake, or they are teased, and suddenly they don't want to perform anymore. I think being nervous is a learned habit, unlike the instinctive fear of snakes or spiders.

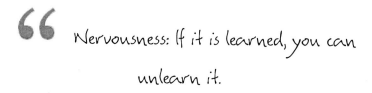

Nervousness: If it is learned, you can unlearn it.

Certainly some of us enjoy the spotlight more than others. We differ in personalities and styles. You might be introverted or extroverted, analytical, or emotion-driven. You might be a novice getting ready to give your first business presentation, or someone who has years of experience. Anyone can get nervous, and in fact most of us do at one point or another. That said, here are some of the best ways to re-think nervousness or stage fright:

Your body responds to any stressful situation. When you are preparing to deliver a presentation, you are like a downhill ski racer standing at the top of the hill; your body provides a shot of adrenaline to give you power. When you race down the hill, you use that adrenaline for speed and control. But when you are speaking, you need to stand still, keep a clear head, and appear calm. When we label this feeling negatively, we feel it as nervousness. When we choose to experience it as—*and call it*—*power,* we can begin to accept it.

Being unprepared increases anxiety. Even though time is in short supply for most of us, adequate preparation will help you avoid anxiety and help you perform at your best. Find time to work through your content until you understand it thoroughly, and then take time to practice it out loud several times. If possible, gather a small group to rehearse with, so you can gain familiarity and fluency with the content.

Lack of experience increases nervousness. Maybe you don't have many opportunities to speak to groups. Maybe you used to present more often than you do now, and your skills are rusty. If you don't get to present very often, volunteer to speak. Choose to get involved in an organization you feel strongly about—your professional organization, a special non-profit, or your condo association. Volunteer speaking can help you build skills as well as confidence, and many people find it a safe space to practice and grow.

Most nervousness does not show. You may feel your knees shaking, your voice quivering, and a bead of perspiration on your upper lip, but your audience often doesn't even notice. I see it all the time in doing video reviews: your perception is often completely different than what the audience sees. You can see for yourself by using video feedback to determine what shows, and what doesn't. You might be pleasantly surprised.

Now that you have had a chance to think about why we get nervous, and to realize most of the time the nervousness just doesn't show, you may be wondering, *"OK, now what do I do about it? Because I know I am still going to get nervous."*

Of course you are going to feel the adrenaline. But the question is: how are you going to turn it to energy and power?

The Inner Game: Changing your thoughts and beliefs

Recognize it. How do you experience nervousness? Take note of what is going on inside your brain and in your body.

- Do you feel butterflies in the pit of your stomach?
- Are your thoughts frantically flying around your head?
- Do you feel tightness in your chest?
- Are you experiencing negative thoughts and self-doubt?

Notice these thoughts and feelings without judgment. Often it is the judgment itself that makes us feel so bad. You might be able to acknowledge the feelings without judgment by thinking, *"Oh, there you are again. Thanks for sending me so much power."*

Accept it. If fear of public speaking is the number one fear, as we often hear, you might as well accept it as being normal. The adrenaline is there for a good reason: to sharpen your wits and prepare you for the action. Since you aren't doing anything dangerous like fighting off a saber-tooth tiger, you interpret the adrenaline as nervousness.

Instead, see if you can simply accept the gift of adrenaline for what it is, your body pumping you up for success. (And maybe you can skip the extra cup of coffee, since caffeine on top of adrenaline is too much of a good thing.)

> " The adrenaline is there for a good reason: to sharpen your wits and prepare you for performance.

Visualize success. I know we are masters of visualization, usually able to envision any number of disasters happening during our presentation. Turn that ability to good by imagining wonderful things happening; your audience loves you, they laugh at your jokes, and applaud you spontaneously. They throw flowers on the stage when you speak. They line up to congratulate you. *You are awesome.* Okay, it might not happen just like that, but instead of imagining disaster, why not imagine success? Enjoy the positive feelings, and carry them with you when you speak.

Use positive self-talk. The little voice inside your head will keep whispering about how unprepared you are, how nervous you feel, or how bored your audience will be. If you notice this negative self-talk, refuse to listen. It's far better to nourish yourself with positive self-talk, like *"I am well-prepared, and excited to meet my audience."* Don't worry if you don't believe it at first, or if it feels contrived and phony. Keep repeating the positive self-talk until it drowns out the negative.

Have realistic expectations. The presentation might not be perfect, or go exactly as you had hoped, but you can still be successful. Set a specific goal you want to accomplish. Choose something you can measure, and that you have control over. For example, if I want my audience to be engaged, my goal might be to conduct an interactive discussion in the first ten minutes of my presentation. That way I can be successful without expecting everything to be perfect.

Level the playing field. Have you ever heard the advice to "imagine your audience in their underwear?" I think it means not letting your audience intimidate you, but engaging them on a personal basis. How? You might move away from a lectern to get physically closer to your audience. You could ask them a few questions to engage them in dialog. You could choose examples and stories that relate to their industry or work. You could even get them on their feet, doing a skit or role-play. See what I mean? Get closer to them in every way you can.

Turn it to POWER. "I feel nervous" is a low-power belief. Just thinking it can make you feel uncomfortable, scared, or vulnerable. If the nervousness you feel is caused by adrenaline, you might as well call it what it is: power. Saying to yourself, "I have the power I need today," feels different, and leads to different thoughts. *Try it yourself. I think you will begin to feel the power.*

> " Instead of imagining disaster, why not imagine success? Enjoy the positive feelings, and carry them with you when you speak.

The Outer Game: changing your physical response

B-r-e-a-t-h-e. When we are under attack, or feel we are, our breathing tends to become rapid and shallow. Or we hold our breath. When we feel the anxiety associated with presenting, neither of these helps us feel better or perform better. In fact, remembering to slow your breath might be just what you need to alleviate nerves. Focusing on your breathing calms you, takes your mind off your worry, and brings oxygen to your brain. What could be better?

Walk it off. If you have tons of physical energy, so much that you have trouble standing still during your presentations, consider burning up some of that physical energy ahead of time. Do a workout, take a swim, or walk down the hallways (or outside if you can) for a few minutes before your presentation. Swing your arms, breathe deeply, and enjoy the sensation of moving. That easy feeling should remain with you as you begin your presentation, and it may reduce your tendency to pace randomly during your presentation.

Shake it out. If you feel tight and tense, especially in your arms, shoulders, or face, take a few moments to loosen up in private before your presentation. Flap your arms, shrug your shoulders, or just shake out your arms and hands. Be silly while you are at it; loosen the mood as well as your body.

Use progressive relaxation. This is helpful if you feel tightness in your shoulders, arms, or even your face. Wherever you find tension, increase it, and then release it. For example, many of us carry tension in our shoulders. If you notice this, shrug your shoulders up around your ears as high as you can, hold a moment, then release. Many professional speakers and actors do stretches to relax their faces before a performance; imagine making a face like a lion roaring.

The Practical Approach: Steps to take

Be better prepared. It's only natural. If you don't know your content thoroughly, of course you will be uncomfortable. Become a subject matter expert on your content by researching, preparing, and rehearsing your talk. Whether you have one day or six months to prepare, start as soon as you can. Read all you can on the topic. Talk about it with others to deepen your knowledge, and to practice your words.

Gather not only statistics, but also stories that bring the content to life. Practice your presentation with a pilot group. Soon you will feel like an expert, and confidence will increase.

Get more practice. Many people present just once or twice a year—no wonder they feel nervous; they just aren't getting enough practice time. It is important for you to practice. Volunteer to speak at your monthly status meetings, offer to train a class on a topic you know well, or become involved in your professional organization where you will present frequently. Also, consider every phone call, meeting, or face-to-face conversation a chance to practice your speaking skills. The more you practice each element, and the more you build each skill and habit, the less you have to worry about.

Join Toastmasters. Toastmasters International is a non-profit organization for people who want to improve their presentation skills. Through member clubs, people work together to improve their communication and leadership skills, and find the courage to change. Before joining, look into local groups in your community or even at your workplace, and visit a time or two to see how you "fit."

Start a practice group. You might not have time or interest in a formal group, so start your own informal network of two or more people who work together to build and reinforce presentation skills. Find people who support you, and who will take time to preview your presentations, and give you honest, useful feedback. Each time you offer feedback, you increase your own awareness and confidence.

What's next?

Right now, pick one to three of these ideas you believe will be most helpful. Create an action plan using the form below, and create a reminder for yourself so you will see it, and act on it each time you speak.

In addition, you may want to create an affirmation, a positive growth statement you can say to yourself any time you notice nerves or negative chatter.

> ❝ Positive affirmations can be extremely powerful; with enough repetition our subconscious begins to believe and act accordingly. ❞

Create an action plan

Design your personal action plan for confidence. Choose actions that will help with your individual concerns. For example, if you have noticed negative internal feedback, make it a goal to provide positive affirmations and feedback to yourself. List one to three concrete steps you feel will help you build confidence.

Your action plan for confidence:

1. _____
   _____

2. _____
   _____

3. _____
   _____

Create an affirmation

Select three words you would like to use to describe yourself as a speaker. This creates a positive mental image of how you want to see yourself as a successful presenter. Write your statement in the present tense. Read or say this affirmation any time you need a boost of confidence and focus.

Example: *"I am a presenter who is calm and confident, fluent in choice of words, and who can easily respond to questions and challenges."*

Your affirmation for confidence:

_____

_____

_____

Chapter Recap:

1. Nervousness before public speaking is perfectly normal, and most of us have experienced it at one time or another. Please don't beat yourself up over it.
2. Instead of trying to "get rid of" adrenaline, transform it into *power and focus*.
3. Create an action plan and affirmation for success, and remember to use them.
4. Always breathe to calm and focus your mind and body.

Chapter 8: Find Your Presentation Strengths

D an was a marketing specialist in a downtown law firm. I met him when he walked into the workshop I was about to facilitate. He was full of smiles and confident body language, and I thought, *"This is going to be a fun session with him in it. He just radiates power and confidence."* A few minutes later, I received a shock. When he walked to the front of the room to introduce himself to the group, he faded before my eyes. His chest sunk, his head bent downward, his voice became very soft and hesitant, and I couldn't see his eyes at all. What a transformation. Every bit of his power was momentarily lost.

Luckily, I had videotaped each participant's introduction. When Dan saw his video, he was surprised, too. It was clear that his personality was not shining through. On the next video recording, I suggested he stand up straight, look audience members right in the eye, and project his energy outward toward them. When he did, he was immediately transformed, back to his confident, powerful self. In the blink of an eye he had reclaimed his personal power. You can do it too.

Discover your delivery strengths

In order to build confidence and power, you will want to begin to understand your own strengths. When we say strengths, we are talking about those qualities or behaviors that seem to come easily to you, and seem to stay the same over time. For example, you may have a gift for telling stories or jokes, while someone else might have the ability to make a complex topic clear. Strengths are so ingrained in our everyday behavior, and come so naturally, you might overlook yours. Because they tend to endure over time, if you are willing to reflect a bit, you might be able to trace yours back to an early age.

To find your strengths, do a little excavating.

- What speaking situations went well for you, and what was unique to that situation?
- Which presentations went so well they seemed effortless?
- What have people often told you about your communication and your presentations?

If you have a chance, video one of your presentations or virtual meetings, and watch or listen so you can understand your unique strengths.

If you still can't see your positive attributes, ask for some help to get more perspective. A friend, a trusted colleague, or a coach can be extremely helpful in this exercise. Look for someone who can offer helpful, balanced feedback. Make sure that person understands you are sincere in seeking to understand your strengths.

" Getting clear on your strengths is not always easy—but it's essential to speaking with authority and genuine power.

When you know your strengths, consider how you can showcase those gifts in your presentations. You'll speak with a more natural, unique style, and you will feel more confident. This is far more powerful than just focusing on fixing your shortcomings.

Take a moment now to capture what you are thinking about your strengths, and how you can play them up. For example, if you:

- Are a gifted storyteller, build stories and vignettes into your talks to illustrate your points.
- Have a dry sense of humor, use it to connect with the audience, or to break the ice.
- Have a strong physical presence, don't hide behind a lectern, or hold your hands together when you speak.
- Are a great conversationalist, create discussions in place of lectures.

Assessing your presentation strengths

Strength or Positive Attribute	Evidence of this Strength	Plan to Showcase this Strength

Checking for weaknesses or blind spots

Joe was a confident young professional, just starting out in his career. He was asked to speak frequently to clients who were invariably more seasoned than he was. His role was that of an educator and advisor, there to help his clients make business decisions based on long-term market trends.

He was so focused on getting his facts straight that he spoke rapidly, in a monotone voice, and with absolutely no passion or excitement about what he was recommending. As a result, he looked uncommitted and unpersuasive.

It wasn't easy for Joe to watch his video. But once he could "see" that he was lacking power and conviction, he started moving away from his dense, content-crowded slides, and started engaging his listeners in conversations about his recommendations. As a result, Joe found his sweet spot, and it was exactly the polar opposite of his lecturing style.

So, like Joe, you will want to be aware of weaknesses or "blind spots," those things you aren't aware of that could be working against you. Where do you feel less than confident? What do you fear or dislike about your speaking skills? What have others told you to work on?

Be sure your assessment is accurate. How have you come to that conclusion—was it something you were told, something you could see on video, or just a perception you have? Is it realistic to think you can change this aspect of your communication? Or do you need to accept it or find a way to work around it?

> **❝** To build your authentic style, focus more on showcasing your strengths than worrying about your weaknesses. Use your strengths to compensate for any weaknesses.

Assessing your presentation blind spots

Concern	Evidence of this weakness (how do you know?)	How easily can it be changed? Is it worth the effort to change?	Action plan to accept, change, or use a strength to compensate

What habits express confidence and power?

Whether you are a novice presenter, or one with years of experience, if you lack self-awareness, you could be undermining your speaking success. Do you come across as weak? Unsure? Or overly confident? Harsh? Unfeeling? A successful speaker blends calm, confidence and warmth properly and authentically.

Get some feedback by asking a trusted colleague, coach, or by seeing yourself on video. Watch for these skills and habits that project confidence and credibility:

Solid stance. Stand firmly on both feet, looking strong, balanced, and steady. Common errors include pacing, shifting or rocking from foot to foot; all of these signal discomfort.

Relaxed but assertive posture. Stand tall, with your shoulders relaxed, your rib cage held up from your waist, and your head steady, not tipped or nodding. This stance should feel relaxed but alert, and it signals strength and composure.

Relaxed hand positions. Keep your hands as natural and open as you can, not locked together, folded across your chest, or jammed into your pockets. You may choose to rest them at your sides or at your waist, but keep them loose and ready for gesturing.

Expressive voice. Breathe and relax your voice. Speak with enough volume and enunciation to be heard and understood. An instant voice improvement: open your mouth a little bit wider for more volume and clarity. Finish each sentence with full volume and a firm downward inflection.

Neutral and appropriate facial expressions. Your facial expression should be relaxed, somewhat neutral. You will also want to look for facial appropriateness—a smile when greeting, a serious look for serious content. Avoid facial habits that look like anger or fear. For example, you might be frowning in concentration, but your audience perceives anger or disapproval.

Direct eye contact. Steady eye contact directs your energy outward, and signals "confidence." Move your eyes slowly and steadily around the room, looking at each person in the audience for one to four seconds before moving on to the next person.

- Avoid letting your eyes dart from one person to the next.
- Avoid making eye contact with only one or two people.
- If eye contact seems difficult or distracting, look at each listener's left eyebrow: to them it looks just like direct eye contact.

As you assess your skills and habits, looking for strengths and weaknesses, what stands out the most?

_____

_____

_____

Which skills and habits do you need to build to maximize your confidence and power?

_____

_____

_____

Which habits do you want to change or eliminate? Remember you will be more successful changing a habit if you replace it with something else. So, for example, if you need to stop saying "um" too much, replace it with a silent pause, and focus on becoming comfortable with the pauses.

_____

_____

_____

Chapter Recap:

1. We all have communication strengths on which we can capitalize, but we may not be aware of what they are. Find and celebrate your own strengths, and use them to your advantage.
2. We all have communication weaknesses that we may not be aware of. Find a coach or trusted colleague to help you identify them. You may be able to correct some weaknesses, or modify your habits. Others you may need to accept or work around.
3. Try to be aware of your strengths and weaknesses without judgment. Everyone is different, and you are fine the way you are.

Chapter 9: Deliver with Style

Lynn attended a conference last year for professionals in her field. The conference was loaded with pertinent breakout sessions, all of which sounded interesting. As she walked along the hallway in front of the breakout rooms, she glanced into each room, trying to decide which session to attend. She noticed one presenter sitting behind a table, not engaging the participants as they entered the room. Another speaker looked disheveled, with a rumpled suit and untrimmed hair. Others struck her as being "too young" or "too old." One stood near the door, smiling and greeting people as they arrived. This was the session Lynn eventually chose to attend.

Clearly, Lynn was basing her decision on first impressions, and as you can imagine, they are not always accurate. Has that ever happened to you? If it has, you know the power of first impressions.

Our brains process many details simultaneously in order to form a first impression—and most people agree it takes just a few seconds. We know instinctively that first impressions are powerful, and yet, if we are too focused on our content or our own nervousness, we can fail to consider the impression we make on others.

> **"** Most agree it takes only a few seconds to form a first impression. Be self-aware, build positive speaking habits, and work to remain calm and open.

Know what impression you are making

Are you aware of the impression you make when you walk into a meeting? Stand up to speak? Enter a social gathering? While many factors are out of your control, it makes sense to be aware of and to control what you can. For example, you may not be able to instantly change your age, body shape, or personality, but you can control a great many of your speaking behaviors.

Let's explore your current skills and habits, deciding what to keep and enhance—and what to improve or downplay.

Posture and Stance:

Are you timid, stage-shy, and uncomfortable? Or are you knowledgeable, confident, and composed? The way you stand tells the audience a lot about you even before you speak. Here are the basic guidelines:

Stand tall. Imagine a string coming out of the top of your head, connecting you to the ceiling. Now imagine what this does to your body language and posture. Your head should be straight, not tipped or tilted toward the floor. Your shoulders should be relaxed. Your ribcage should be lifted slightly, enough to let you breathe properly, but not enough to put tension or stiffness in your shoulders or back.

Plant your feet. With your feet apart, distribute your weight evenly on both feet, feeling the balance point about at your waistline. In this position you should feel grounded and secure. Watch newscasters and professional speakers; they rarely sway or rock. Be sure to keep your feet apart, not tightly together or crossed.

66 Adopt a "Power Pose" that helps you look—and feel—confident every time you speak.

Check for tension. The most common tension points when presenting are often your shoulders, arms, neck and face. Tension in these areas will cause you to look stiff and uncomfortable, or serious and too formal. Before you begin, shrug and relax your muscles all the way from your shoulders to your fingertips.

Stand still. Shifting or rocking can make you look too casual, cocky, or nervous. If you tend to shift frequently, or step from one foot to the other, put your feet a little wider apart, or place one foot in front of the other. You don't have to stand rock-still for a long time, but it's best to start and end in a calm, centered way.

Great delivery rests on the fine balance between using your energy, and letting it run wild. While you don't want to be frozen into one position for your entire presentation, you shouldn't be pacing or wandering aimlessly around the room either.

> " Choose to move by choice, not by habit, and stop moving when you get where you are going.

Gestures and Hand Positions:

One of the most common presentation worries is: what on earth do I do with my hands when I speak? While we rarely think about our hands when we are having conversations, or going about our day, when we stand up to speak, suddenly we don't know what to do with them.

Poor hand positions can make a poor first impression, since we tend to do them when we are uncomfortable, often during the first minute or two of our presentations. Whenever your hands and your words are incongruent, you send a confusing or negative message. For example, if you say, *"I am happy to be here,"* with your hands folded across your chest, the listener might assume that you are not happy at all.

When you are aware of the risks, you can make better choices and better first impressions.

Risky hand positions:

Fig leaf. When we lock our hands together below the waist, we lose our power, and look weak, uncomfortable, intimidated, or fearful. Our energy is trapped, and we look constricted. As a result we gesture very little or not at all.

In your pockets. This feels comfortable, so it's a hard habit to break. Despite how it feels, it looks unprofessional, and you will end up not gesturing when you should. Or you will gesture with your hands in your pockets, not an attractive look. In some cultures, it is considered rude to speak with your hands in your pockets even during informal conversations. Worst of all, with your hands in your pockets, you don't look open or engaged. Break this habit as soon as you can.

Behind your back. When you put your hands behind your back, your energy often goes right to your feet, and you end up pacing, shifting, or rocking from side to side. Because you can't gesture with your hands behind your back, you don't look open or engaged. It's best to avoid this position.

Folded across your chest. Ah, that feels good. Too good. Since we know it looks "closed" and standoffish, let's don't even go there.

On your hips. This is a powerful body language, one that says, *"I am in charge here."* Use it with extreme care, maybe with a rowdy group that needs to be reined in, but not your boss's boss, clients or in the boardroom.

Better hand positions:

At your sides. This classic "neutral" position looks great, although it feels somewhat vulnerable, and you may not like how it feels at first. From this position your hands are in a readiness position, which means you might gesture more. If you make this choice, be sure to relax your shoulders, arms and hands, so it looks natural, not forced.

At your waist in the steeple position. Bring your hands together loosely at your waist, with your fingertips just touching one another. This position feels natural instantly for many people. Keep your hands relaxed, not locking them or fidgeting. The steeple position automatically looks confident and may lead you to gesture more successfully.

Doing something productive. Holding the slide advancer or laser pointer, making effective gestures, showing a prop, passing out handouts, or writing on a flip chart. Using your hands naturally means you don't need to think so much about them. Much better. Try to have something productive to keep your hands from being a worry.

" By understanding hand positions and their risks and benefits, you can make better choices about what to do with your hands—which means you can focus on your content and your audience.

Speaking with your hands:

People often explain that they are concerned about their hand gestures. Someone has told them they speak with their hands too much. They become self-conscious about gesturing. Yes, gestures have a bad reputation, and one that is often *not deserved.*

In fact, gestures serve a very useful purpose in our speaking: they express, emphasize, and enhance the meaning of our words. They bring energy and passion into our presentations. When they match our speech, they add credibility to our delivery.

So how do we take advantage of hand gestures? It is easier to gesture when you start with your hands in a neutral position, at your sides or at your waist. That makes it easier for you to spontaneously use your hands to "paint a picture" of what you are saying.

Because it is difficult to plan a gesture and have it look natural, your best bet may be to "allow" gestures, rather than force them.

Here are best practices to help you make the most of your gestures:

Keep your hands relaxed. If you put your hands in your pockets, clasp them behind your back, or lock them into a fig-leaf position, chances are you will not use them effectively. Start with your hands relaxed and at your sides, and you'll be more likely to gesture.

Let it happen. When you say, "It's over there," your hand may begin to move "over there." Let it go. Allow the gesture to last a little longer, and make it a little larger for even more impact.

Visualize it. If you can see something in your mind, you can probably use gestures to help describe it. Picture the roller coaster, and you are more likely to describe it with your hands.

Use more space. Making small, tight gestures with your hands and arms close to your sides, say "low power, low confidence." Expansive gestures say "confident!" Try to move your elbows away from your body for a more powerful gesture.

Trust video feedback. Don't automatically believe it when someone says you use your hands too much. You may be using gestures beautifully—until you hear this comment and stop using your hands at all. Video feedback, or the advice of someone you trust, can help you decide how your gestures look.

> " If you tend to use gestures freely, make it a habit to keep your feet still, which balances your high energy with stillness.

Reduce mannerisms. Mannerisms like playing with a pen or touching your face can be very distracting. Video feedback can help you build awareness of these habits, so you can reduce or eliminate them.

Voice Quality and Habits:

Did your mother or father ever tell you to "speak up" or "enunciate?" Good advice, because voice is critical to your image. An expressive, animated voice adds color and emotion to your words, while a flat, monotonous voice makes even a well-crafted presentation seem lifeless. And if we can't hear your voice because it is too soft…well, that's not good. To make the most of your voice, practice positive vocal habits like these:

Relax your voice. Breathe. Sip lukewarm liquid. Do not clear your voice repeatedly, or you will make matters worse. Good news: the strain in your voice is almost always more obvious to you than it is to your audience.

Improve a flat or soft voice. Try opening your mouth wider to increase volume. You may have tension in your face, so try relaxing your jaw by gently massaging right in front of your ears. Open your mouth and yawn softly. Keep breathing.

Project your voice. You can learn to project your voice without straining it by breathing from the diaphragm. Practice speaking while lying down, using your abdominal muscles to project your voice to the ceiling. As you return to an upright position, try to keep speaking from your abdomen, not just from your mouth or throat.

Eliminate "up-speak." If you end sentences with upward inflections, you sound like you are asking questions, and that makes you sound *uncertain*. For more credibility, your statements should have a firm, downward inflection.

Reduce vocal fillers. Since most verbal fillers like "um" and "so" seem to creep in between sentences, substitute a pause. It will take some concentration to become comfortable with pauses, but it will sound just right to your listeners. Stay focused on what you are saying, not what is on the next slide, so you are less distracted.

Record yourself when you are on the telephone, in meetings, or in casual conversations. When you listen to your voice, pay attention to filler words, and then work to reduce them in everyday speaking situations.

> " Clear speech sets you apart from the crowd, especially over the telephone or in virtual presentations—and with practice and feedback you can master vocal skills.

Facial Expressions:

Our faces often reflect our feelings. Anxiety, fear, indifference, passion, commitment—what message do you intend to send? Make sure your face reflects the content and tone of your presentation, rather than your internal thoughts and worries.

As you become more aware and more flexible in using facial expressiveness, it will become another element to convey meaning and emotion. Here are some ways to build "facial fluency":

Keep it relaxed. Breathe and relax your face. Check a mirror to see if there is tension in your face, especially in your eyebrows, forehead, between your eyes, or around your mouth. If you see tension, keep breathing, and try again to relax your face into a more neutral expression.

Smile. Many of us think we are smiling when we are not. Take time at the beginning of each presentation to greet your audience with a smile. This loosens up your face, and releases some of the tension you may be feeling.

Keep it appropriate to your tone and message. When you are greeting your audience or speaking on a positive subject, a smile is appropriate. When you have a serious or negative message, a neutral or thoughtful look will be a better choice. Ideally your face will reflect your message.

Get feedback. Ask someone you trust to watch your face while you speak, and then give you feedback. Or video your presentation and watch it, taking note of your facial expressions. Recording your face while you are speaking on a conference call will give you valuable feedback so you can be aware of your facial expressions.

> ❝ Don't let habits like smiling too much or frowning constantly undermine you—be conscious of your facial expressions, and vary them according to your message.

Maximizing Eye Contact:

Eye contact is one of the most important skills in public speaking, but it is often overlooked. Even experienced speakers can ignore this critical skill. Great eye contact provides a powerful connection with your audience, and signals confidence and credibility. Begin today to build these eye contact habits:

Keep it steady. Maximize the amount of time you spend looking at your audience while minimizing the amount of time you are looking anywhere else. Don't read from your notes, stare at your visuals, or look at the floor, the ceiling, or an invisible dot on the back wall. Don't dart or skate around the room, because *the goal is to connect.*

Aim for one to four seconds. Many speakers find it easy to scan the audience, but they find it more challenging to extend eye contact to a few seconds. However, most audiences will say they appreciate getting that much eye contact. With a little practice, eye contact should feel as if you are having a mini-conversation with every person in your audience, one person at a time.

Avoid a staring contest. You might find yourself staring at the one friendly face in the room, the top-ranking audience member, or the person who is most likely to challenge you. It's better to keep your eye contact moving slowly around the room, including everyone, one person at a time.

Remember the back of the room. People who sit in the back of the room, or off to the sides, often receive less eye contact. If you are aware of this tendency, you can be sure to include them. Observe the room before you begin, and stand where you can easily connect with people in every part of the room.

Maintain room control. Keep an eye on your audience at all times, and don't turn away from them. Deliberate, steady eye contact may help you keep side conversations and disruptions to a minimum. It should help everyone stay tuned in.

Dress for Success:

What's your image? And does it even matter? What you choose to wear, and how you wear it, can be an enhancement or a distraction when you present. By choosing clothing and accessories appropriate to the occasion, as well as ones that make you feel great, you increase your odds of success. Here are five "rules" for dressing for success:

Dress up slightly. By dressing appropriately, matching your audience, or going slightly more formal, you show respect and signal your professionalism. You also enjoy a greater sense of self-confidence. If your work requires a uniform or work clothes, dressing up might mean changing into dress shoes, or adding a simple jacket or sports coat.

Count on comfort. No matter how attractive your clothing is, if you keep tugging or pulling to keep it in place, you will not present confidence or credibility. Nothing should bind or restrict your movement, so only wear what fits properly. Also, make sure your shoes are comfortable if you will be standing for your presentation.

Trust the tried-and-true. Your old standby is safer than something new, especially when you get a rude surprise when a button pops off, the fabric wrinkles, or you realize you forgot to remove one of the tags. Wear everything at least once before the big presentation.

Check the condition. Plan ahead to be sure what you plan to wear is clean and pressed, and your shoes and other accessories are in good condition. Check for loose buttons and hems. All your accessories including handbags, backpacks, watches or computer bags are part of your image, so be sure they are appropriate and professional.

Stick with simple and professional. Avoid busy prints, jangling jewelry, hair that falls across your face or anything else that distracts. Keep your look simple and clean so listeners remember what you said, not what you wore. Even if the setting is casual, you should always appear professional.

> " Select your attire deliberately, be sure you are well-groomed, and that your clothing is comfortable and appropriate.

Assess your delivery skills

Ah, the moment of truth. You understand which delivery skills signal calm strength, and why those skills and habits are so important to build and practice. But as my colleague and friend Jane says, *"There is a big difference between knowing and doing. Seeing myself on video was just what I needed, and I'm now a big fan of videoing my practice sessions."*

So let's see how you measure up. Find a presentation you are currently working on, or a presentation you gave previously. Stand and deliver the presentation in an empty room, or if possible, to a small group of listeners. Record your presentation, using a video camera, your smartphone or a voice recorder. Watch and/or listen to see how you actually come across.

> If you find it challenging to evaluate your skills accurately, enlist a trusted colleague or a presentation coach to help you see what is already working—and what could be better.

Use our comprehensive feedback sheet to help you consider the various aspects of your presentation skills. Using your phone's camera scan the link below to download your free copy of the feedback sheet.

Applause Feedback Sheet

Chapter Recap:

1. Great delivery skills and habits are made with self-awareness and practice, and are not something you need to be born with. Learn to observe and improve your skills and habits without being hypercritical.
2. How you stand, how you move, the expressions on your face, and how you use your voice and eye contact for impact—these all make an important difference in how your audience sees you.
3. With patience and persistence you can change habits and build skills that allow you to focus on your audience and your message, instead of worrying about how you look and sound.

Chapter 10: Speaking Virtually Via Technology

Jason remembered his very first virtual presentation—at least the first minute of it. As the new lead person on a process-improvement initiative, he had worked hard to be well prepared. He knew what he was going to say, had practiced with the technology, and was comfortable with how it worked. What he was completely unprepared for was the silence—and no human faces in front of him. Even though he knew his content well, he froze for what seemed like long minutes. Finally he spoke his first words, and after a few long, painful minutes, he seemed to regain his composure.

During our Train the Trainer workshop, Jason asked the other trainers in the room to brainstorm strategies to cope with virtual settings. Once Jason understood the dynamics of virtual presentations, he was better equipped to maintain his focus, and speak in a friendly, conversational style.

Some things we seem to learn the hard way, but you don't have to add virtual presentations to the list.

Because the dynamics of virtual meetings are so different from live meetings, we need to adapt our style to make this new format a highly engaging experience. Here are some tips Jason used to begin making the most of virtual presentations—and he now says his virtual presentations are sailing along nicely.

Remember your voice is critical. Since the listeners can't see you, all they have to go on are your voice and your slides (if you are using them). If you don't know how your voice sounds, now is the time to get a voice recorder so you can record and listen to yourself. This may not be your idea of fun, but it is definitely an eye-opener, so listen for these subtle but significant aspects of voice control:

- How many "ums" and "ahs" do you hear?

- Is your voice expressive, or monotone?

- Do you have good volume?

- Do you enunciate clearly, or do you mumble?

- Do your sentences drop off at the end, sound like questions, or do they end with power?

- How is the voice quality over the phone line or headset you plan to use?

> " If you found opportunities for voice improvement, working on them now will pay dividends for years.

A great way to stretch your vocal range is to periodically record yourself in a practice presentation, exaggerating each aspect of enunciation, inflection, rate of speech, etc. Think of how broadcast announcers put life and color into their voices. Imagine yourself speaking with enthusiasm, selling your message. Exaggerate each aspect of your vocal expression. When you listen, see if those exaggerated vocals were as over-the-top as you felt, or if they actually added value to your speaking.

Don't use a script unless absolutely necessary. Your audience will be able to tell whether you are reading or speaking. Instead of a script, choose to use notes with key words or bullets that will allow you to speak in a more conversational way.

Rehearse your content, as much or more than you would for a live presentation. Pay particular attention to the opening minutes, the transitions between topics, and the closing. Ask a person or a small group to listen and give you feedback, or record yourself and play it back so you can hear for yourself.

Engage the audience in the first three minutes. If you don't engage the audience until midway through your presentation, they will be used to *listening*, and won't respond as well as they would have in the first few minutes. Ask them to introduce themselves by writing on the virtual white board, if time and the group size permit. If you know your audience, do a quick "check-in" with each person as they arrive for the meeting. Keep asking them questions, or asking them to take actions, such as "write this down." The more you can keep them engaged, the better.

Have an assistant. Have an assistant in the room with you, or on the phone with you, so you can "talk" to him or her. You will experience less of that "blind" feeling you can get when you don't see an audience. In addition, an assistant can manage audience questions or any technology issues, allowing you to focus on your content and delivery. Your assistant can work next to you—or virtually.

Keep the group small. If the group is small and they know one another, you can make the call much more personal. This intimacy may keep people from drifting in and out of attention. There is nothing more engaging than hearing your name called with a comment or question attached. Your audience may stay focused if they think you might call on them.

If the group is large, privatize the chat function. In a large group, or when listeners don't know one another, there is a reluctance to speak up or ask a question. If you keep the chat and question function anonymous, only you and your assistant can see the questions. You can encourage people to ask anything they want, because they will remain anonymous. This should reduce the fear of asking a "dumb" question, and you can respond to comments or questions when you choose to.

Post pictures. Put pictures of people where you can see them as you speak. Make these the happiest-to-see-you faces you can. Or post pictures of your pets or loved ones, if this helps you feel more connected to someone or something that makes you smile.

Sit up. Move your laptop or monitor to a chest-high shelf so you aren't looking down into the camera. This lets you keep your head raised, and your breathing natural, and you will get a more attractive video and voice production.

Stand up. This allows you to breathe more deeply, and puts more energy in your voice. Use a good-quality headset/microphone so the sound stays consistent as you move around.

Open your mouth wider. Enunciate carefully. This can keep you from rushing your words, and make you more easily understood. Don't be afraid to pause periodically, and keep breathing.

Smile. Yes, we can hear a smile in your voice.

Take a moment to apply these ideas to your virtual meetings or presentations:

What I need to remember for a successful virtual meeting/presentation:
1.
2.
3.
4.
5.
6.

Chapter Recap:

1. Speaking with a remote audience is becoming more common, so you will benefit by building skills and confidence with this format.
2. Rehearse every aspect of virtual presentations so that you know it will go well, and you can keep your focus on your listeners and the important content you have to share with them.
3. Your virtual presentations will be far more successful if you can engage your audience through questions, stories, or using their names when appropriate, making them more likely to stay on the call.

Conclusion: Bring Out Your Best

You have been on quite a journey to build the confidence, skills, self-awareness and habits you need to become the speaker you always wanted to be. Are you there yet? Or are you still being tough on yourself, and frustrated because you aren't "perfect"?

Here are some of the key insights I hope you have come to appreciate:

You will never be perfect. You said "um" too many times. You didn't tell that illustrative story as well as you did during your rehearsal. You failed to answer a question as succinctly as you had hoped you would. Oh well, that's presenting. You may have an occasional flash of brilliance, or a moment when everything seems perfect, but most of the time there will be a few flaws in your presentation.

> How to tell if you have become a more effective speaker: did you get your point across? Did you make a difference to your audience? If you did, then you were successful.

You can keep growing. It's okay to let these little mistakes go, and think no more of them. Don't dwell in the land of negativity. But, look for trends, and act on them. For example, if you frequently or consistently fail to answer a question as well as you could, it's a signal to continue working on your skills and habits in responding to questions. Don't be negative about it; just give it some attention before your next presentation. Or practice these skills during everyday meetings and phone conversations.

You can keep fine-tuning. We can only focus on a few things at a time. When we are presenting we have many balls to juggle: the content, the slides, the technology, the delivery, the audience, and the questions that might arise. Whew! Work on just one or two improvements at a time. Build those new skills, and reinforce those new habits. Periodically review the aspects of presenting to see what new skills on which you need to focus. This keeps you fresh and continuously challenged. Much better than sitting back and thinking, "It's no use, I'm terrible," or "I'm good enough already."

So what can you do to see yourself as the skilled speaker you are? If you have been reluctant to video yourself, perhaps now is the time. Then watch the video, using the checklist provided to analyze your skills and habits.

Continuous Improvement Check-in

How have your presentation skills developed from where you started? How have you changed?

What do you appreciate about yourself as a speaker?

What skills do you want to build next?

What things don't you like? Can you change them, work around them, or accept them as part of who you are?

Forgiveness and encouragement

What would you tell a good friend if she came to you for advice about her presentation skills, or anything else for that matter? You would tell her *not to be so hard on herself.* You would point out her strengths, and focus on them. You would encourage her to build one or two new skills to get even better, and you would remind her how capable she is—and that you believe in her.

Yes, you would encourage your friend, but how do you talk to yourself? We are sometimes very unforgiving of ourselves, when in fact we would never treat a friend or colleague the same way. *Please talk encouragingly to yourself* by creating a new, updated affirmation.

Take a moment now to create your new affirmation:

My Skilled-Speaker Affirmation

Even though I have been hard on myself in the past, I am becoming an encouraging coach to myself. I am proud of myself for working hard to become a more skilled speaker. As I continue to build and refine my skills and habits, I notice that I am continually improving in my ability to _____, _____, and _____.

How did that affirmation feel? Good, I hope. It's exactly what a good friend or coach would say to encourage you. How wonderful it is when you can encourage yourself.

If you had a difficult time with this exercise, or if you really don't feel you have been able to build the skills and confidence you want, no matter how hard you have tried, please consider professional coaching.

What can a presentation coach do for you?

Give unbiased feedback. Your colleagues or bosses may be too close or too critical to be unbiased. A coach has a different relationship with you, and no agenda other than to help you get better.

Build your confidence. A good coach can help you see you at your best, and help you recognize your strengths as well as weaknesses, helping you put them in perspective.

Ask you good questions. A coach can help you develop good content, using questions to see if your logic and conclusions are sound, your data is solid, and your message is on target.

Stretch you. You may feel silly trying something new, but you might find that what the coach encourages you to try makes all the difference in the world. You probably wouldn't have tried it on your own.

Help you see what others see. Speaking in front of the mirror can't give you this valuable feedback. Ask your coach to video you, and help you see your strengths as well as weaknesses.

What is coaching like?

Different coaches have different approaches, but if you and I were beginning a coaching relationship, I would start by asking you about the following:

- Your previous experience or any training you have had in presentations or public speaking.
- Your current presentations, and the challenges you face in presenting. Why this is important now.
- What conditions have led you to be successful, and what situations caused you to struggle.
- Your goals and your time frame to make these changes happen.
- How you plan to measure your success.

In addition to meeting your developmental goals, we would likely begin working on a real presentation or speaking situation so we would have content to focus on during our sessions. Some people like to work on a past presentation, but I would encourage you to work on a future one—the stakes are higher, and your motivation to address the content is stronger.

Together, we would brainstorm to determine your purpose for the presentation, and craft your Targeted Message.

- You would then practice your presentation, both with and without visuals, while I video record it.
- Together, we would review the video to assess your delivery skills and habits, and to determine what is working, and what could be better.

- We might refine your content by adding a stronger opening or closing, or by inserting a great story to bring your content to life.
- We would prepare you for challenging questions from your listeners.
- Then we would repeat the process, focusing on those areas where you want to refine the presentation, or where you want to focus on a particular element or skill.

If you are interested in working with a presentation coach, here are some questions to ask:

1. Does the coach have any certification or training in coaching?

2. How much coaching experience does the coach have?

3. What is the process this coach follows?

4. What results might you expect?

5. How much time does the coach feel it will take?

6. What follow-up will you receive?

7. Is video recording and playback included?

8. Where, how often, and how long are the coaching sessions?

9. Who has this coach worked with, and can you get references?

10. What will the fee be? When and how will you be asked to pay?

Final words

I sincerely hope your journey has been a positive and productive experience for you. From my years working with coaching clients and workshop attendees, I know that public speaking is a source of worry, doubt and frustration. It doesn't have to be that way. As you develop both skills and self-confidence, presenting becomes a doable challenge and a source of pride.

Keep going, keep growing, and keep encouraging yourself. And be sure to celebrate what you have accomplished. Please drop me a line and let me know how your presentations are going.

Take a bow because now *you are an exceptional presenter*. Here's to you, and to presentations so good you deserve applause!

About the Author

Gail Zack Anderson, President of Applause, Inc. leads workshops and provides individual coaching to help people who struggle to find their confidence, and who find it difficult to organize their thoughts and words. No matter what you do, if speaking clearly and confidently is a critical skill, she can help you master it.

For the past 25 years Gail has partnered with people from a range of organizations and functions, helping them to create compelling content and deliver meetings, training, or presentations with confidence and credibility.

Gail has a MA in Human Resource and Change Leadership from the University of St. Thomas, and a BS in Business from the University of Minnesota. Gail has served on the board of directors and is a past president for ATD-GTC.